Textured Stitches

KNITTED
SWEATERS
& ACCESSORIES
with
smart details

Connie Chang Chinchio

INTERWEAVE
interweave.com

EDITOR Ann Budd

TECHNICAL EDITOR Lori Gayle

ART DIRECTOR Liz Quan

COVER AND
INTERIOR DESIGN Julia Boyles

PHOTOGRAPHY Joe Hancock

WARDROBE, HAIR,
AND MAKEUP Jessica Shinyeda

ILLUSTRATIONS Gayle Ford

PRODUCTION Katherine Jackson

Interweave Press LLC
201 East Fourth Street
Loveland, CO 80537-5655 USA
Interweave.com

Printed in China by C&C Offset

Library of Congress
Cataloging-in-Publication Data

Chinchio, Connie Chang.
Textured stitches : knitted sweaters and
accessories with smart details / Connie
Chang Chinchio.
  p. cm.
Includes index.
ISBN 978-1-59668-316-7 (pbk.)
1. Knitting--Patterns. I. Title.
TT825.C394 2011
746.43'2041--dc23
2011017159

10 9 8 7 6 5 4 3 2 1

Acknowledgments

The process of writing a book with twenty designs is a huge undertaking for someone used to churning out one design at a time, and I am extremely grateful for the help and support I received along the way. Foremost, I'd like to thank my wonderful sample knitters—Alyssa Kabel, Angela Hahn, Cecily Glowik MacDonald, Elspeth Kurth, Melissa Wehrle, and Virginia Lawther. In particular, Angela, Cecily, and Melissa set aside time from their own hectic design schedules to help out a friend, and for that I am indebted to them. Their eagle eyes and vast experience caught many a bug in the instructions before a single stitch was even cast on: their generosity and talent spoiled me.

I'd also like to thank my infinitely patient editors, Anne Merrow, who started this journey with me, and Ann Budd, who helped me complete it. They were always available to lend a critical eye and words of encouragement when my energy flagged. Thanks also go to my technical editor, Lori Gayle, who worked quickly, efficiently, and accurately. I'd also like to thank Joe Hancock for his stunning photographs, Julia Boyles for the beautiful design of the book, and Liz Quan for overseeing it all.

Finally, I'd like to thank my family—Maurizio and Olivia—without whom none of this would have any meaning. Maurizio is the best sort of fiber husband—patient, kind, encouraging—though very eager to reclaim his home after nearly a year buried under yarn and sketches for this book. Our daughter, Olivia, and this book gestated at the same time—I discovered that I was pregnant right after the project list was finalized. And so it is to her that I dedicate this book. I hope to share my love of knitting with her and dare to dream that someday she may even knit some of these designs.

Contents

Introduction

When I was seven, my grandmother introduced me to knitting in a desperate attempt to keep an overly talkative and inquisitive child quiet. Fascinated by the fabric that grew out of manipulating a series of loops and string on two needles, I found myself irrevocably addicted. In those first months, I patiently made an endless series of blankets and scarves out of mammoth skeins of multicolored yarn I found buried in the craft bins at the local Woolworth's. Eventually bored with what I thought were the limits of my knitting abilities, I set it aside for many long years.

It wasn't until my second year of graduate school that, gripped by the desire to craft something handmade and personal for my then-boyfriend/now-husband, I picked up needles again. I was living in Ithaca, New York, at the time—a small town that prides itself on handicrafts and natural materials, as well as two yarn shops. My first forays into those yarn shops introduced me to the dizzying possibilities of yarn and fiber. Colors and plies and composition—there were countless variations to satisfy any appetite. Although I was drawn mostly to natural fine-gauged fibers with a tight twist—yarns that I found to be durable, versatile, and easy to wear—my head could be easily turned by a soft hand-dyed, single-ply beauty. After a few unfortunate missteps, I eventually learned which yarns were appropriate for which situations (100% angora, for example, made a very poor pair of socks).

There were other valuable lessons I learned during my first years of truly obsessive knitting. I learned that I preferred to buy yarn locally where I could touch, see, and yes, even smell yarn before I made a commitment. I found that colors that appeared so entrancing on my computer monitor might be muddier, pinker, darker, or lighter when viewed in person. I learned that circular needles put less strain on my arms than straight needles and that the magic-loop method of knitting meant that longer circular needles were more versatile than shorter ones. Most importantly, I learned that I didn't have to follow a pattern to the letter, that I could adjust certain elements to fit my particular shape.

My first love was, and still is, stockinette stitch, that perfect companion to the classic, unfussy sweaters that I adore; sweaters that are equally at home in the office or on an evening out. But it wasn't long before I discovered that the judicious addition of texture patterns—achieved by the simple combination of knit-and-purl-stitch building blocks, sometimes incorporating a few artfully placed yarnover increases and directional decreases—could make a garment truly special. And I learned that texture stitches could also be used to help shape a garment—a tight cabled pattern could cinch in a waist: a lacy pattern could add width and movement to a hem.

This book includes some of my explorations of ways in which textured stitch patterns can add aesthetics and structure in knitted garments. For variety, I've included small, simple accessories such as headbands, gloves, and hats that can be whipped out in an afternoon or two, despite my predilection for fine yarns, as well as full-size garments such as pullovers, cardigans, hoodies, and Henleys that require more commitment, but whose results I hope you'll find well worth the extra time. Let *Textured Stitches* inspire you to play with texture the next time you pick up your needles.

Caitlin
CABLED SCARF

I love the look of thick cabled scarves—especially when they're generous enough to wrap several times around my neck. For scarves, it's important to choose a yarn that's soft enough to wear against the skin and hardy enough for everyday use. Both soft and lofty, Quince and Company's Osprey is ideal for this densely cabled scarf. Interlocking cables meander along the length, but the stitch pattern is actually quite easy to memorize. After several repeats, you'll find yourself putting away the chart and simply reading the stitches as you go.

FINISHED SIZE
About 10½" (26.5 cm) wide and 67" (170 cm) long, after blocking.

yarn
Worsted weight (#4 Medium).

SHOWN HERE: Quince and Company Osprey (100% wool; 170 yd [155 m]/100 g): lichen, 4 skeins.

needles
U.S. size 9 (5.5 mm).

Adjust needle size if necessary to obtain the correct gauge.

notions
Cable needle (cn); tapestry needle.

gauge
20 sts and 24½ rows = 4" (10 cm) in cable patt from chart.

Scarf

CO 52 sts. Rep Rib Rows 1 and 2 of Cable chart until piece measures 3" (7.5 cm) from CO when stretched to 10½" (26.5 cm) wide, ending with WS Rib Row 2. Work Rows 1–36 of chart 10 times (do not rep the rib rows), then work Rows 1–14 once more—374 rows completed from main section of chart. Rep Rib Rows 1 and 2 until piece measures 3" (7.5 cm) long when stretched to 10½" (26.5 cm) wide (i.e., work the same number of rows as at the beg). Loosely BO all sts.

Finishing

Block lightly. Weave in loose ends.

	knit on RS; purl on WS
·	purl on RS; knit on WS

3/3RC: sl 3 sts onto cn and hold in back, k3, k3 from cn

3/3LC: sl 3 sts onto cn and hold in front, k3, k3 from cn

Cable

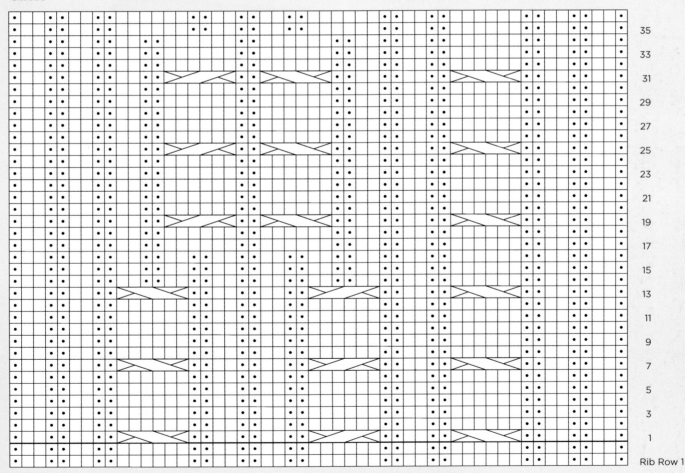

Professoressa
CARDIGAN

Generous front bands featuring argyle motifs give a vaguely professorial look to this lightweight cardigan. The small gauge of the cozy alpaca blend makes it possible to accommodate the large-scale argyle pattern without overwhelming the rest of the garment. Long, flared balloon sleeves and body shaping speak to a different sort of drama. The front bands are knitted simultaneously with the body, which is worked in a single piece. The front bands extend into the collar, which is shaped with short-rows and simple ribbing to help it hug the neck.

FINISHED SIZE

About 32 (34¾, 38¾, 43, 47¼, 51¼)" (81.5 [88.5, 98.5, 109, 120, 130] cm) bust circumference, with front edges overlapped by about 1" (2.5 cm).

Sweater shown measures 34¾" (88.5 cm).

yarn

Sportweight (#2 Fine).

SHOWN HERE: Berroco Ultra Alpaca Light (50% alpaca, 50% wool; 144 yd [133 m]/50 g): #4282 boysenberry mix, 8 (9, 10, 11, 11, 12) skeins.

needles

BODY AND SLEEVES: U.S. size 5 (3.75 mm).

NECKBAND: U.S. size 4 (3.5 mm).

Adjust needle sizes if necessary to obtain the correct gauge.

notions

Markers (m); stitch holders; cable needle (cn); tapestry needle.

gauge

23 sts and 32 rows = 4" (10 cm) in St st on larger needles.

29 sts of Right and Left Band charts measure 3¾" (9.5 cm) wide on larger needles.

NOTES

» The lower body is worked in one piece to the armholes, then divided for working the fronts and back separately to the shoulders.

Body

With larger needles, CO 204 (220, 244, 268, 292, 316) sts.

ROW 1: (RS) Work Row 1 of Right Band chart (see page 15) over 29 sts, place marker (pm), k26 (30, 36, 42, 48, 54) right front sts, pm for right "seam," sl 1 purlwise with yarn in back (pwise wyb), pm, k92 (100, 112, 124, 136, 148) back sts, pm for left "seam," sl 1 pwise wyb, pm, k26 (30, 36, 42, 48, 54) for left front, pm, work Row 1 of Left Band chart (see page 15) over 29 sts.

ROW 2: (WS) Work next row of Left Band chart over 29 sts, slip marker (sl m), *knit to m before "seam" st, sl m, p1, sl m; rep from * once more, knit to last 29 sts, work next row of Right Band chart over 29 sts.

ROW 3: (RS) Work next row of Right Band chart over 29 sts, knit to last 29 sts (slipping m as you come to them), work next row of Left Band chart over 29 sts.

ROWS 4–12: Rep Rows 2 and 3 four more times (do not rep Row 1), then work WS Row 2 once more—6 garter ridges outside cable patts and slipped seam sts; piece measures 1" (2.5 cm) from CO in garter st sections.

Change to working garter sts in St st and pm for darts on next row as foll:

NEXT ROW: (RS) Work 29 chart sts, sl m, k8 (10, 14, 17, 21, 24), pm for right front dart, k18 (20, 22, 25, 27, 30), sl m, sl 1 pwise wyb, sl m, k18 (20, 22, 25, 27, 30), pm for right back dart, k56 (60, 68, 74, 82, 88) center back sts, pm for left back dart, k18 (20, 22, 25, 27, 30), sl m, sl 1 pwise wyb, sl m, k18 (20, 22, 25, 27, 30), pm for left front dart, k8 (10, 14, 17, 21, 24), sl m, work 29 chart sts.

Cont chart patts and slipped seam sts as established, work rem sts in St st until piece measures 3¼" (8.5 cm) from CO, ending with a WS row.

DEC ROW: (RS) Cont cable patts and seam sts as established, work to 2 sts before right front dart m, k2tog, sl m, work to right back dart m, sl m, ssk, work to 2 sts before left back dart m, k2tog, sl m, work to left front dart m, sl m, ssk, work to end—4 sts dec'd.

[Work 7 rows even, then rep the dec row] 4 times—184 (200, 224, 248, 272, 296) sts rem. Work even until piece measures 10" (25.5 cm) from CO, ending with a WS row.

INC ROW: (RS) Work to right front dart m, M1 (see Glossary), sl m, work to right back dart m, sl m, M1, work to left back dart m, M1, sl m, work to left front dart m, sl m, M1, work to end—4 sts inc'd.

[Work 9 rows even, then rep the inc row] 4 times—204 (220, 244, 268, 292, 316) sts. Removing dart m on next row, work even until piece measures 16" (40.5 cm) from CO for all sizes, ending with a WS row.

	knit on RS; purl on WS
ℓ	k1tbl on RS
•	purl on RS; knit on WS
	sl 1 st onto cn and hold in back, k1tbl, p1 from cn
	sl 1 st onto cn and hold in front, p1, k1tbl from cn
	sl 1 st onto cn and hold in back, k1tbl, k1tbl from cn
	on RS: sl 1 st onto cn and hold in front, k1tbl, k1tbl from cn; *on WS:* sl 1 st onto cn and hold in front, p1tbl, p1tbl from cn

Left Band

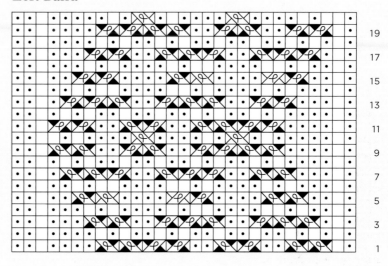

Right Band

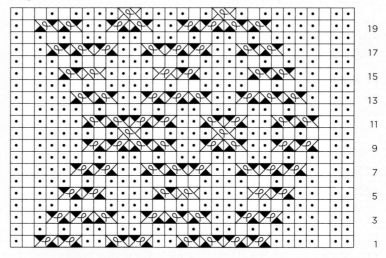

Divide for Fronts and Back

DIVIDING ROW: (RS) Removing seam st m as you come to them, work 52 (55, 60, 65, 69, 73) sts in patt, BO 8 (10, 12, 14, 18, 22) right armhole sts, work until there are 84 (90, 100, 110, 118, 126) back sts on needle after BO gap, BO 8 (10, 12, 14, 18, 22) sts for left armhole, work to end—52 (55, 60, 65, 69, 73) sts rem for each front; 84 (90, 100, 110, 118, 126) sts rem for back. Break yarn and place back and left front sts on separate holders.

Right Front

With WS facing, join yarn to 52 (55, 60, 65, 69, 73) right front sts at armhole edge. Work 1 WS row even.

ROW 1: (RS) Work 29 chart sts, sl m, k1, ssk (neck dec), work to last 3 sts, k2tog (armhole dec), k1—2 sts dec'd; 1 each at neck and armhole.

ROWS 2 AND 4: (WS) Work even in patt.

ROWS 3 AND 5: Work 29 chart sts, sl m, work to last 3 sts, k2tog, k1—1 st dec'd at armhole only in each row.

ROW 6: Work even in patt.

Rep these 6 rows 0 (0, 1, 2, 2, 3) time(s), then work the first 4 (4, 2, 0, 2, 0) rows once more—45 (48, 50, 53, 55, 57) sts rem; armhole shaping is complete. Cont in patt, dec 1 st at neck edge as established (i.e., every 3rd RS row) 4 (5, 4, 6, 5, 5) more times—41 (43, 46, 47, 50, 52) sts rem. Work even as established until armhole measures 7 (7½, 8, 8½, 9, 9)" (18 [19, 20.5, 21.5, 23, 23] cm), ending with a WS row. Place 12 (14, 17, 18, 21, 23) St st shoulder sts on one holder, then place 29 chart sts on separate holder to work later for back neckband.

Left Front

Return 52 (55, 60, 65, 69, 73) held left front sts to larger needles. With WS facing, rejoin yarn at left front edge. Work 1 WS row even.

ROW 1: (RS) K1, ssk (armhole dec), work to last 32 sts, k2tog (neck dec), k1, sl m, work 29 chart sts—2 sts dec'd; 1 each at neck and armhole.

ROWS 2 AND 4: (WS) Work even in patt.

ROWS 3 AND 5: K1, ssk, work in patt to end—1 st dec'd at armhole only in each row.

ROW 6: Work even in patt.

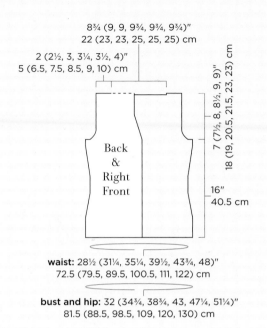

8¾ (9, 9, 9¾, 9¾, 9¾)"
22 (23, 23, 25, 25, 25) cm

2 (2½, 3, 3¼, 3½, 4)"
5 (6.5, 7.5, 8.5, 9, 10) cm

7 (7½, 8, 8½, 9, 9)"
18 (19, 20.5, 21.5, 23, 23) cm

Back
&
Right
Front

16"
40.5 cm

waist: 28½ (31¼, 35¼, 39½, 43¾, 48)"
72.5 (79.5, 89.5, 100.5, 111, 122) cm

bust and hip: 32 (34¾, 38¾, 43, 47¼, 51¼)"
81.5 (88.5, 98.5, 109, 120, 130) cm

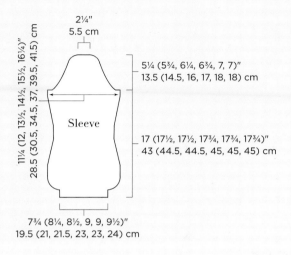

2¼"
5.5 cm

Sleeve

11¼ (12, 13½, 14½, 15½, 16¼)"
28.5 (30.5, 34.5, 37, 39.5, 41.5) cm

5¼ (5¾, 6¼, 6¾, 7, 7)"
13.5 (14.5, 16, 17, 18, 18) cm

17 (17½, 17½, 17¾, 17¾, 17¾)"
43 (44.5, 44.5, 45, 45, 45) cm

7¾ (8¼, 8½, 9, 9, 9½)"
19.5 (21, 21.5, 23, 23, 24) cm

Rep these 6 rows 0 (0, 1, 2, 2, 3) time(s), then work the first 4 (4, 2, 0, 2, 0) rows once more—45 (48, 50, 53, 55, 57) sts rem; armhole shaping is complete. Cont in patt, dec 1 st at neck edge as established (i.e., every 3rd RS row) 4 (5, 4, 6, 5, 5) more times—41 (43, 46, 47, 50, 52) sts rem. Work even as established until armhole measures 7 (7½, 8, 8½, 9, 9)" (18 [19, 20.5, 21.5, 23, 23] cm), ending with a WS row. Place 12 (14, 17, 18, 21, 23) St st shoulder sts on one holder, then place 29 chart sts on separate holder to work later for back neckband.

Back

Return 84 (90, 100, 110, 118, 126) held back sts to larger needles. With WS facing, rejoin yarn to armhole edge. Work 1 WS row even.

DEC ROW: (RS) K1, ssk, work to last 3 sts, k2tog, k1—2 sts dec'd.

[Work 1 WS row even, then rep the dec row] 4 (4, 6, 8, 9, 11) times—74 (80, 86, 92, 98, 102) sts rem. Work even until armholes measure 1 row short of 7 (7½, 8, 8½, 9, 9)" (18 [19, 20.5, 21.5, 23, 23] cm) and contain 1 row less than front armholes, ending with a RS row.

NEXT ROW: (WS) P12 (14, 17, 18, 21, 23), BO center 50 (52, 52, 56, 56, 56) sts, purl to end—12 (14, 17, 18, 21, 23) sts rem for each shoulder; armholes measure same as fronts. Place sts on separate holders.

Sleeves

With larger needles, CO 45 (47, 49, 52, 52, 55) sts. Work in garter st (knit every row) for 14 rows, ending with a WS row—7 garter ridges; piece measures 1¼" (3.2 cm) from CO. Knit 1 RS row, inc 24 (24, 24, 25, 31, 30) sts evenly spaced—69 (71, 73, 77, 83, 85) sts. Work even in St st until piece measures 5¼" (13.5 cm) from CO for all sizes, ending with a WS row.

DEC ROW: (RS) K1, ssk, work to last 3 sts, k2tog, k1—2 sts dec'd.

[Work 7 rows even, then rep the dec row] 4 (4, 3, 3, 3, 2) times—59 (61, 65, 69, 75, 79) sts rem. Work even until sleeve measures 11¾ (12¼, 12, 11, 11, 11)" (30 [31, 30.5, 28, 28, 28] cm) from CO, ending with a WS row.

INC ROW: (RS) K1, M1, knit to last st, M1, k1—2 sts inc'd.

[Work 11 (11, 7, 7, 7, 7) rows even, then rep the inc row] 2 (3, 5, 6, 6, 6) times—65 (69, 77, 83, 89, 93) sts. Work even in St st until piece measures 17 (17½, 17½, 17¾, 17¾, 17¾)" (43 [44.5, 44.5, 45, 45. 45] cm) from CO, ending with a WS row.

Shape Cap

BO 5 (6, 7, 8, 10, 12) sts at beg of next 2 rows—55 (57, 63, 67, 69, 69) sts rem.

DEC ROW: (RS) K1, ssk, work to last 3 sts, k2tog, k1—2 sts dec'd.

Rep the dec row every RS row 4 (5, 7, 8, 8, 8) more times, then every other RS row (i.e., every 4th row) 4 (4, 3, 3, 3, 3) times, then every RS 6 (6, 8, 9, 10, 10) times—25 sts rem for all sizes. Work 1 WS row even. BO 3 sts at beg of next 4 rows—13 sts rem. BO all sts.

Finishing

Block pieces to measurements. With RS touching and WS facing outward, use the three-needle method (see Glossary) to BO 12 (14, 17, 18, 21, 23) front and back sts tog at each side—29 neckband sts rem on holder for each front. With yarn threaded on a tapestry needle, sew sleeve seams. Sew sleeve caps into armholes.

Back Neckband

NOTE: The neckband is worked in rib patt using short-row shaping so it hugs the back of the neck.

Right Neckband

Place 29 held right neckband sts on smaller needles. With RS facing, join yarn at center front edge.

ROW 1: (RS) P2, [k1, p1] 12 times, k2tog, k1 (seam selvedge st; knit every row)—28 sts rem.

ROW 2: (WS) K1 (seam selvedge), [p1, k1] 12 times, p1, k2.

ROW 3: P2, [k1, p1] 12 times, k2.

Work short-rows (see Glossary) as foll:

SHORT-ROW 1: (WS) Work as established to last 6 sts, wrap next st, turn work.

SHORT-ROWS 2 AND 4: (RS) Work in patt to end.

SHORT-ROW 3: Work as established to last 11 sts, wrap next st, turn.

SHORT-ROW 5: Work as established to last 16 sts, wrap next st, turn.

SHORT-ROW 6: Work in patt to end.

SHORT-ROW 7: (WS) Work to end of row, working wraps tog with wrapped sts.

SHORT-ROW 8: (RS) Work 1 row even across all sts.

Rep the last 8 short-rows 2 more times. Work even as established until neck edge of band (beg of WS rows; end of RS rows) reaches to center of back neck when slightly stretched. Place sts on holder.

SHORT-ROW 7: (RS) Work to end of row, working wraps tog with wrapped sts.

SHORT-ROW 8: (WS) Work 1 row even across all sts.

Rep the last 8 short-rows 2 more times. Work even as established until neck edge of band (end of WS rows, beg of RS rows) reaches to center of back neck when slightly stretched. Place sts on holder. Block neckbands, if desired.

With RS touching and WS facing outward, use the three-needle method to BO the 28 neckband sts tog. With yarn threaded on a tapestry needle, sew neck edge of joined bands to back neck.

Weave in loose ends.

Left Neckband

Place 29 held left neckband sts on smaller needles. With WS facing, join yarn at center front edge.

ROW 1: (WS) K2, [p1, k1] 12 times, p2tog, k1 (seam selvedge st; knit every row)—28 sts rem.

ROW 2: (RS) K1 (seam selvedge), [k1, p1] 12 times, k1, p2.

ROW 3: K2, [p1, k1] 13 times.

Work short-rows as foll:

SHORT-ROW 1: (RS) Work as established to last 6 sts, wrap next st, turn.

SHORT-ROWS 2 AND 4: (WS) Work in patt to end.

SHORT-ROW 3: Work as established to last 11 sts, wrap next st, turn.

SHORT-ROW 5: Work as established to last 16 sts, wrap next st, turn.

SHORT-ROW 6: Work in patt to end.

Lustro
CARDIGAN

Worked in a lustrous blend of silk and wool, the cables at the yoke of this open-front cardigan stand out in plump definition. Subtle body shaping enhances the fit, while rolled edges keep the overall look casual and comfortable. This cardigan is worked in pieces and seamed to support the shape of the luxurious, but heavy, yarn. The lower body and sleeve cuffs are worked in reverse stockinette to help the edges lie flat. Feel free to fasten the fronts with a pretty shawl pin if you prefer more coverage.

FINISHED SIZE

About 31 (34, 37½, 41, 44½, 49)" (78.5 [86.5, 95, 104, 113, 124.5] cm) bust circumference.

Cardigan shown measures 34" (86.5 cm).

yarn

DK weight (#3 Light).

SHOWN HERE: Louisa Harding Grace Wool & Silk (50% merino, 50% silk; 110 yd [101 m]/50 g): #22 reflection (light blue), 10 (11, 12, 13, 14, 14) skeins.

needles

U.S. size 6 (4 mm).

Adjust needle size if necessary to obtain the correct gauge.

notions

Markers (m); stitch holders; cable needle (cn); tapestry needle.

gauge

22 sts and 31 rows = 4" (10 cm) in St st.

26 sts in cable patts of Right and Left Cable Panel charts average 4" (10 cm) wide.

NOTES

» During front armhole shaping, if there are not enough stitches to work a complete 3- or 4-stitch cable, work the stitches in stockinette instead.

» The front bands and back collar are not shown on the schematic.

» As an alternative to seaming the front bands to the front edges, they can be joined to the fronts as they are knitted by working a band edge stitch together with 1 stitch picked up from the front edge. To prevent the front bands from stretching, join each band with a ratio of 3 band rows for every 4 front rows in the stockinette section of the body. Join 1 band row for every front row in the cabled yoke.

Back

CO 85 (93, 103, 113, 123, 135) sts.

ROW 1: (RS) K1, purl to last st, k1.

ROW 2: (WS) Knit.

ROW 3: Rep Row 1—piece measures about ½" (1.3 cm), including the CO row.

ROW 4: K1 (selvedge st; knit every row), purl to last st, k1 (selvedge st; knit every row).

ROW 5: Knit.

Rep Rows 4 and 5 (do not rep Rows 1–3) until piece measures 4½" (11.5 cm) from CO, ending with a RS row.

Shape Waist

Place dart markers (m) as foll:

NEXT ROW: (WS) K1, p16 (17, 19, 21, 23, 26), place marker (pm), p51 (57, 63, 69, 75, 81) center sts, pm, p16 (17, 19, 21, 23, 26), k1.

DEC ROW: (RS) Knit to m, slip marker (sl m), ssk, knit to 2 sts before next m, k2tog, sl m, knit to end—2 sts dec'd.

[Work 7 rows even, rep dec row] 3 times—77 (85, 95, 105, 115, 127) sts rem. Work even until piece measures 9" (23 cm) from CO, ending with a WS row.

INC ROW: (RS) Knit to m, sl m, M1 (see Glossary), knit to next m, M1, sl m, knit to end—2 sts inc'd.

[Work 9 rows even, rep inc row] 3 times—85 (93, 103, 113, 123, 135) sts. Work even until piece measures 15½" (39.5 cm) from CO, ending with a WS row.

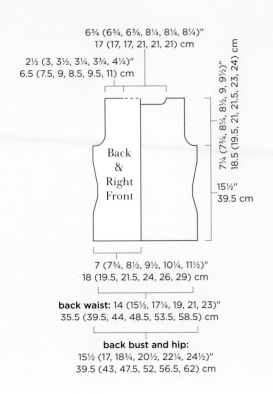

6¾ (6¾, 6¾, 8¼, 8¼, 8¼)"
17 (17, 17, 21, 21, 21) cm
2½ (3, 3½, 3¼, 3¾, 4¼)"
6.5 (7.5, 9, 8.5, 9.5, 11) cm
Back & Right Front
7¼ (7¾, 8¼, 8½, 9, 9½)"
18.5 (19.5, 21, 21.5, 23, 24) cm
15½"
39.5 cm
7 (7¾, 8½, 9½, 10¼, 11½)"
18 (19.5, 21.5, 24, 26, 29) cm
back waist: 14 (15½, 17¼, 19, 21, 23)"
35.5 (39.5, 44, 48.5, 53.5, 58.5) cm
back bust and hip:
15½ (17, 18¾, 20½, 22¼, 24½)"
39.5 (43, 47.5, 52, 56.5, 62) cm
2¼"
5.5 cm
11½ (12½, 13¼, 14¼, 15, 16¼)"
29 (31.5, 33.5, 36, 38, 41.5) cm
Sleeve
5¼ (5¾, 6¼, 6¾, 7¼, 7¾)"
13.5 (14.5, 16, 17, 18.5, 19.5) cm
17½ (17½, 17½, 17¾, 17¾, 17¾)"
44.5 (44.5, 44.5, 45, 45, 45) cm
8¼ (9, 9, 9¾, 10, 10¼)"
21 (23, 23, 25, 25.5, 26) cm

Shape Armholes

BO 5 (5, 6, 7, 8, 9) sts at beg of next 2 rows—75 (83, 91, 99, 107, 117) sts rem.

DEC ROW: (RS) K1, ssk, knit to last 3 sts, k2tog, k1—2 sts dec'd.

Resume working selvedge sts in garter st, rep dec row on the next 4 (5, 6, 8, 9, 12) RS rows—65 (71, 77, 81, 87, 91) sts rem. Work even until armholes measure 6¼ (6¾, 7¼, 7½, 8, 8½)" (16 [17, 18.5, 19, 20.5, 21.5] cm), ending with a WS row.

Shape Neck

With RS facing, k16 (19, 22, 20, 23 25), BO center 33 (33, 33, 41, 41, 41) sts, knit to end—16 (19, 22, 20, 23, 25) sts rem each side.

NOTE: The shoulder widths do not increase all the way up the size range because there are only two back neck widths. The three largest sizes all share the larger back neck, which makes the shoulder width of the fourth size narrower than the shoulder width of the third size.

Place sts for right back neck on holder or allow them to rest on needle while working the left neck.

Left Side

Working 16 (19, 22, 20, 23, 25) left back neck sts only, work 1 WS row even.

DEC ROW: (RS) K1, ssk, knit to end—1 st dec'd.

Rep the last 2 rows once more—14 (17, 20, 18, 21, 23) sts rem. Work even until armholes measure 7¼ (7¾, 8¼, 8½, 9, 9½)" (18.5 [19.5, 21, 21.5, 23, 24] cm), ending with a WS row. Place sts on holder.

Right Side

Return 16 (19, 22, 20, 23, 25) held right neck sts to needle, if they are not already on the needle, and rejoin yarn with WS

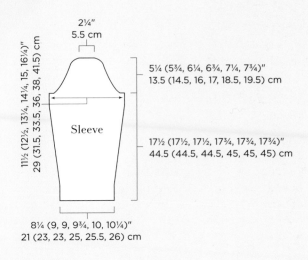

[Work 7 rows even, rep dec row] 3 times—34 (38, 43, 48, 53, 59) sts rem. Work even until piece measures 9" (23 cm) from CO, ending with a WS row.

INC ROW: (RS) Knit to m, M1, sl m, knit to end—1 st inc'd.

[Work 9 rows even, rep inc row] 3 times—38 (42, 47, 52, 57, 63) sts. Work even until piece measures 15¼" (38.5 cm) from CO, ending with a RS row.

Establish Cable Panel and Shape Armhole

NEXT ROW: (WS) K1, p6 (7, 9, 11, 13, 13), [p3, M1] 10 (11, 12, 13, 14, 16) times, k1—48 (53, 59, 65, 71, 79) sts.

NEXT ROW: (RS) K1, work Row 1 of Right Cable Panel chart (page 26) over 42 (47, 53, 58, 63, 74) sts by working the 26 sts before the patt rep box once, then work the 11-st rep 1 (1, 2, 2, 2, 3) time(s), then work 5 (10, 5, 10, 15, 15) sts after patt rep box once to end where indicated for your size; p4 (4, 4, 5, 6, 3), k1—piece measures 15½" (39.5 cm) from CO.

NEXT ROW: (WS) BO 5 (5, 6, 7, 8, 9) sts, work in patt to last st, k1—43 (48, 53, 58, 63, 70) sts rem.

DEC ROW: (RS) K1, work in patt to last 3 sts, k2tog, k1—1 st dec'd.

Resume working selvedge sts in garter st, rep dec row on the next 4 (5, 6, 8, 9, 12) RS rows (see Notes)—38 (42, 46, 49, 53, 57) sts rem. Work even until armhole measures 7¼ (7¾, 8¼, 8½, 9, 9½)" (18.5 [19.5, 21, 21.5, 23, 24] cm), ending with a RS row. Make a note of the last cable chart row completed so you can end the left front with the same row later. Dec as foll to prevent cables from flaring at the shoulder:

NEXT ROW: (WS) P1 (1, 1, 2, 1, 1), [p2tog, p3] 7 (8, 9, 9, 10, 11) times, p2 (1, 0, 2, 2, 1)—31 (34, 37, 40, 43, 46) sts rem.

Place 17 (17, 17, 22, 22, 23) sts at the neck edge on one holder to work later for back collar; place rem 14 (17, 20, 18, 21, 23) shoulder sts on another holder.

Left Front

CO 38 (42, 47, 52, 57, 63) sts. Work as for back until piece measures 4½" (11.5 cm) from CO, ending with a RS row.

facing to neck edge. Work 1 WS row even.

DEC ROW: (RS) Knit to last 3 sts, k2tog, k1—1 st dec'd.

Rep the last 2 rows once more—14 (17, 20, 18, 21, 23) sts rem. Work even until armholes measure 7¼ (7¾, 8¼, 8½, 9, 9½)" (18.5 [19.5, 21, 21.5, 23, 24] cm), ending with a WS row. Place sts on holder.

Right Front

CO 38 (42, 47, 52, 57, 63) sts. Work as for back until piece measures 4½" (11.5 cm) from CO, ending with a RS row.

Shape Waist

Place dart m as foll:

NEXT ROW: (WS) K1, p16 (17, 19, 21, 23, 26), pm, p20 (23, 26, 29, 32, 35), k1.

DEC ROW: (RS) Knit to 2 sts before m, k2tog, sl m, knit to end—1 st dec'd.

Shape Waist

Place dart m as foll:

NEXT ROW: (WS) K1, p20 (23, 26, 29, 32, 35), pm, p16 (17, 19, 21, 23, 26), k1.

DEC ROW: (RS) Knit to m, sl m, ssk, knit to end—1 st dec'd.

[Work 7 rows even, rep dec row] 3 times—34 (38, 43, 48, 53, 59) sts rem. Work even until piece measures 9" (23 cm) from CO, ending with a WS row.

INC ROW: (RS) Knit to m, sl m, M1, knit to end—1 st inc'd.

[Work 9 rows even, rep inc row] 3 times—38 (42, 47, 52, 57, 63) sts. Work even until piece measures 15¼" (38.5 cm) from CO, ending with a RS row.

Establish Cable Panel and Shape Armhole

NEXT ROW: (WS) K1, [p3, M1] 10 (11, 12, 13, 14, 16) times, p6 (7, 9, 11, 13, 13), k1—48 (53, 59, 65, 71, 79) sts.

NEXT ROW: (RS) K1, p4 (4, 4, 5, 6, 3); work Row 1 of Left Cable Panel chart (page 27) over 42 (47, 53, 58, 63, 74) sts beg where indicated for your size by working the 5 (10, 5, 10, 15, 15) sts before the patt rep box once, then work the 11-st rep 1 (1, 2, 2, 2, 3) time(s), then work the 26 sts after the patt rep box once; k1—piece measures 15½" (39.5 cm) from CO.

NEXT ROW: (WS) K1, work in patt to last st, k1.

NEXT ROW: (RS) BO 5 (5, 6, 7, 8, 9) sts, work in patt to last st, k1—43 (48, 53, 58, 63, 70) sts rem.

NEXT ROW: (WS) K1, work in patt to last st, k1.

DEC ROW: (RS) K1, ssk, work in patt to last st, k1—1 st dec'd.

Resume working selvedge sts in garter st, rep dec row on the next 4 (5, 6, 8, 9, 12) RS rows—38 (42, 46, 49, 53, 57) sts rem. Work even until armhole measures 7¼ (7¾, 8¼, 8½, 9, 9½)" (18.5 [19.5, 21, 21.5, 23, 24] cm), ending with the same RS chart row as right front. Dec as foll to prevent cables from flaring at the shoulder:

NEXT ROW: (WS) P2 (1, 0, 2, 2, 1), [p3, p2tog] 7 (8, 9, 9, 10, 11) times, p1 (1, 1, 2, 1, 1)—31 (34, 37, 40, 43, 46) sts rem.

Place 17 (17, 17, 22, 22, 23) sts at the neck edge on one holder to work later for back collar; place rem 14 (17, 20, 18, 21, 23) shoulder sts on another holder.

Sleeves

CO 45 (49, 49, 53, 55, 57) sts. Work as for back until piece measures 2½" (6.5 cm) from CO, ending with a WS row.

INC ROW: (RS) K1, M1, knit to last st, M1, k1—2 sts inc'd.

Rep inc row every 6th row 0 (0, 0, 0, 0, 8) times, then every 8th row 0 (0, 4, 8, 13, 7) times, then every 10th row 0 (4, 7, 4, 0, 0) times, then every 12th row 8 (5, 0, 0, 0, 0) times—63 (69, 73, 79, 83, 89) sts. Work even until sleeve measures 17½ (17½, 17½, 17¾, 17¾, 17¾)" (44.5 [44.5, 44.5, 45, 45, 45] cm) from CO, ending with a WS row.

Shape Cap

BO 5 (5, 6, 7, 8, 9) sts at beg of next 2 rows—53 (59, 61, 65, 67, 71) sts rem.

Legend

□ knit on RS; purl on WS	□ pattern repeat	sl 1 st to cn and hold in back, k2, p1 from cn	sl 2 sts to cn and hold in back, k2, k2 from cn
• purl on RS; knit on WS	sl 2 sts to cn and hold in back, k1, k2 from cn	sl 2 sts to cn and hold in front, p1, k2 from cn	sl 2 sts to cn and hold in back, k2, k2 from cn

Right Cable Panel

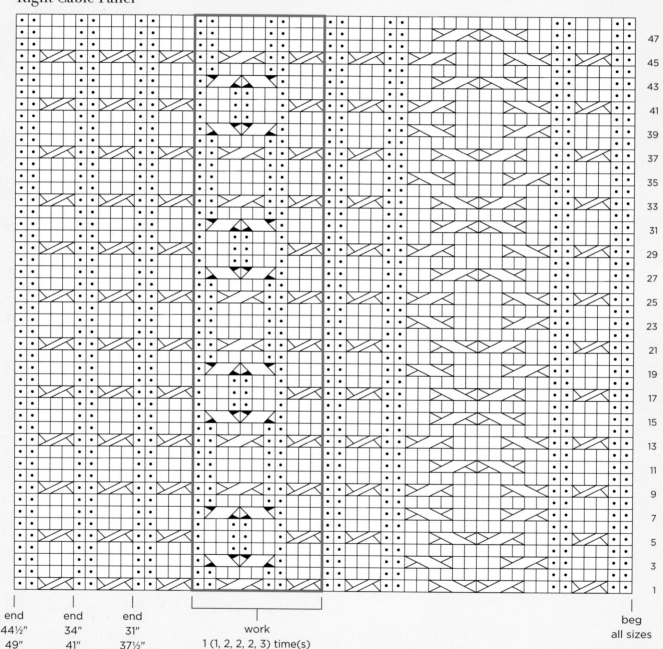

47
45
43
41
39
37
35
33
31
29
27
25
23
21
19
17
15
13
11
9
7
5
3
1

end
44½"
49"

end
34"
41"

end
31"
37½"

work
1 (1, 2, 2, 2, 3) time(s)

beg
all sizes

Left Cable Panel

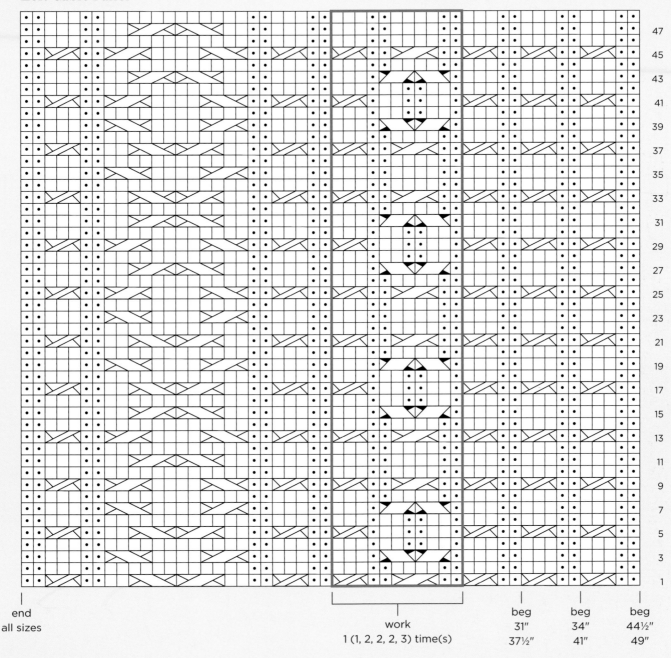

47
45
43
41
39
37
35
33
31
29
27
25
23
21
19
17
15
13
11
9
7
5
3
1

end
all sizes

work
1 (1, 2, 2, 2, 3) time(s)

beg
31"
37½"

beg
34"
41"

beg
44½"
49"

DEC ROW: (RS) K1, ssk, work to last 3 sts, k2tog, k1—2 sts dec'd.

Rep dec row on the next 3 (5, 5, 6, 6, 6) RS rows, then every other RS row (i.e., every 4th row) 4 (3, 4, 4, 5, 6) times, then every RS row 5 (7, 7, 8, 8, 8) times, ending with a dec row—27 (27, 27, 27, 27, 29) sts rem. Work 1 WS row even, then BO 3 (3, 3, 3, 3, 4) sts at beg of next 2 rows, then BO 4 sts at beg of next 2 rows—13 sts rem for all sizes. BO all sts.

Finishing

Block pieces to measurements (see Notes). With RS touching and WS facing outward, use the three-needle method (see Glossary) to BO the 14 (17, 20, 18, 21, 23) front and back St st shoulder sts tog— 17 (17, 17, 22, 22, 23) sts for collar rem on holders at each side.

With yarn threaded on a tapestry needle, sew sleeve caps into armholes, easing to fit. Sew sleeve and side seams.

Right Front Band and Collar

CO 9 sts.

ROW 1: (RS) Purl to last st, k1 (seam st; knit every row).

ROW 2: (WS) Knit.

ROW 3: Rep Row 1—piece measures about ½" (1.3 cm), including the CO row.

ROW 4: K1, purl to end.

ROW 5: Knit.

Rep Rows 4 and 5 (do not rep Rows 1–3) until piece measures same length as right front edge from CO to held collar sts at shoulder when slightly stretched (about 3 front band rows for every 4 St st body rows and 1 front band row for every cable body row), ending with a WS row.

NEXT ROW: (RS) K9 front band sts, return 17 (17, 17, 22, 22, 23) held right front sts to needle with RS facing and knit across them—26 (26, 26, 31, 31, 32) sts total.

NEXT ROW: (WS) K1, purl to end.

NEXT ROW: (RS) Knit.

Rep the last 2 rows once more, ending with a RS row. Shape collar with short-rows (see Glossary) as foll:

SHORT-ROW 1: (WS) K1, purl to last 5 sts, wrap next st, turn work.

SHORT-ROWS 2, 4, AND 6: (RS) Knit to end.

SHORT-ROW 3: K1, purl to last 10 sts, wrap next st, turn work.

SHORT-ROW 5: K1, purl to last 15 sts, wrap next st, turn work.

SHORT-ROW 7: K1, purl to end, working wraps tog with wrapped sts.

SHORT-ROW 8: Knit.

Rep the last 8 short-rows 2 more times. Work even until collar reaches to center back neck, ending with a WS row. BO all sts.

Left Front Band and Collar

CO 9 sts.

ROW 1: (RS) K1 (seam st; knit every row), purl to end.

ROW 2: (WS) Knit.

ROW 3: Rep Row 1—piece measures about ½" (1.3 cm), including the CO row.

ROW 4: Purl to last st, k1.

ROW 5: Knit.

Rep Rows 4 and 5 (do not rep Rows 1–3) until piece measures same length as left front edge from CO to held collar sts at shoulder when slightly stretched (about 3 front band rows for every 4 St st body rows and 1 front band row for every cable body row), ending with a RS row.

NEXT ROW: (WS) P9 front band sts, return 17 (17, 17, 22, 22, 23) held left front sts to needle with WS facing and purl to last st, k1—26 (26, 26, 31, 31, 32) sts total.

NEXT ROW: (RS) Knit.

NEXT ROW: (WS) Purl to last st, k1.

Rep the last 2 rows once more, ending with a RS row. Shape collar with short-rows as foll:

SHORT-ROW 1: (RS) Knit to last 5 sts, wrap next st, turn work.

SHORT-ROWS 2, 4, AND 6: (WS) Purl to last st, k1.

SHORT-ROW 3: Knit to last 10 sts, wrap next st, turn work.

SHORT-ROW 5: Knit to last 15 sts, wrap next st, turn work.

SHORT-ROW 7: Knit to end, working wraps tog with wrapped sts.

SHORT-ROW 8: Purl to last st, k1.

Rep the last 8 short-rows 2 more times. Work even until collar reaches to center back neck, ending with a WS row. BO all sts.

With yarn threaded on a tapestry needle, sew BO edges of right and left collar tog at center back neck. Sew selvedge of collar extensions to back neck edge. Sew selvedges of front bands to body, easing to fit.

Block again, if desired. Weave in loose ends.

Treccia
WRAP

This cozy wrap is worked in a luxurious blend of merino, silk, and cashmere that's sumptuously comfortable against even bare shoulders. The k2, p2 ribbing and cable pattern is reversible, so you'll never have to worry if the "right" side is facing out. Adjust the length of the plain ribbed section to customize the size—longer for a more voluminous wrap or shorter for a lighter cover. For symmetry and neat flexible edges, the scarf begins with a tubular cast-on and ends with a sewn bind-off.

FINISHED SIZE

About 17" (43 cm) wide and 68" (173 cm) long.

yarn
DK weight (#3 Light).

SHOWN HERE: Sublime Cashmere Merino Silk DK (75% merino, 20% silk, 5% cashmere; 127 yd [116 m]/50 g): #0055 blue, 9 skeins.

needles
U.S. size 5 (3.75 mm): 24" (60 cm) circular (cir).

Adjust needle size if necessary to obtain the correct gauge.

notions
Waste yarn for provisional CO; spare cir needle in same size or smaller than main needle for working rounded edge; cable needle (cn); tapestry needle.

gauge
24 sts and 32 rows = 4" (10 cm) in k2, p2 rib.

32 sts = 4" (10 cm) wide in cable patt.

Stitch guide

8/8LC (worked over 16 sts)

Sl 8 sts onto cable needle (cn) and hold in front of work, [k2, p2] 2 times, then work 8 sts from cn as [k2, p2] 2 times.

Cable Motif 1 (worked over 112 sts)

ROW 1: 8/8LC (see above), work 80 sts in established rib patt, 8/8LC.

ROWS 2–20: Work 19 rows even in established rib.

ROW 21: Work 16 sts in rib, 8/8LC, work 48 sts in rib, 8/8LC, work 16 sts in rib.

ROWS 22–40: Work 19 rows even in established rib.

ROW 41: Work 32 sts in rib, 8/8LC, work 16 sts in rib, 8/8LC, work 32 sts in rib.

ROWS 42–60: Work 19 rows even in established rib.

ROW 61: Work 48 sts in rib, 8/8LC, work 48 sts in rib.

Cable Motif 2 (worked over 112 sts)

ROW 1: Work 48 sts in rib, 8/8LC, work 48 sts in rib.

ROWS 2–20: Work 19 rows even in established rib.

ROW 21: Work 32 sts in rib, 8/8LC, work 16 sts in rib, 8/8LC, work 32 sts in rib.

ROWS 22–40: Work 19 rows even in established rib.

ROW 41: Work 16 sts in rib, 8/8LC, work 48 sts in rib, 8/8LC, work 16 sts in rib.

ROW 42–60: Work 19 rows even in established rib.

ROW 61: 8/8LC, work 80 sts in rib, 8/8LC.

NOTES

» Because each row begins with k2 and ends with p2 and because the cables are worked in k2, p2 rib pattern, the wrap is completely reversible. Consequently, the piece does not have a true right or wrong side.

Wrap

Rounded Cast-on

With waste yarn, use a provisional method (see Glossary) to CO 56 sts. Work 4 rows even in St st (knit RS rows; purl WS rows). Carefully remove the waste yarn from the provisional CO and place 56 exposed sts on a spare needle. Fold the St st fabric in half so the RS (knit side) faces outward and the two needles are parallel. Join main yarn. Using one tip of the main needle, work the sts from the other two needle tips onto the main cir needle as foll: *K2 from the front needle, p2 from the back needle; rep from * to the end—112 sts arranged in k2, p2 rib.

Body

Work k2, p2 rib as established (knit the knits, and purl the purls) for 21 rows—piece measures about 2¾" (7 cm) from folded edge of CO. Work Rows 1–61 of Cable Motif 1 (see Stitch Guide). Work even in established rib until piece measures 57¾" (146.5 cm) from CO. Work Rows 1–16 of Cable Motif 2 (see Stitch Guide). Work 21 rows even in established rib—piece measures about 68" (173 cm) from CO. Using the k2, p2 sewn method (see box at right), BO all sts.

Finishing

Weave in loose ends along the sides of knit columns to conceal the ends as much as possible for a reversible wrap.

Block lightly if desired.

K2, P2 Tubular Cast-On and K2, P2 Sewn Bind-Off

The tubular cast-on and its matching sewn bind-off result in nice professional-looking edges that are both stretchy and flexible. These edges can be worked for any rib multiple (for example, k1, p1; k2, p2; k3, p3) as long as the number of knit stitches equals the number of purl stitches. The instructions here are for a k2, p2 rib.

K2, P2 Tubular Cast-On

STEP 1: With waste yarn, use a provisional method (see Glossary) to cast on half the desired number of stitches. For the Treccia Wrap, which calls for 112 stitches, you will provisionally cast on 56 stitches.

STEP 2: Work 4 rows even in stockinette stitch (knit right-side rows; purl wrong-side rows) to form the double-knit section of the ribbed edging.

STEP 3: Carefully remove the waste yarn from the provisional cast on and place the exposed live stitches onto a knitting needle. Fold the piece so that the needles are parallel and the right sides (the knit sides) of the piece face outward and the wrong sides (the purl sides) face together. In this orientation, one needle will be behind the other and the business ends of the needles will be aligned.

STEP 4: With a third needle, *knit 2 stitches from the front needle, then purl 2 stitches from the back needle; repeat from * until all stitches have been worked—there will now be the desired number of stitches (112 stitches) on the third needle and they will be arranged in k2, p2 rib.

Continue to work piece as desired.

K2, P2 Sewn Bind-Off

STEP 1: Work k2, p2 rib for desired length.

STEP 2: Work 4 rows even as foll:

Knit the knit stitches and slip the purl stitches purlwise while holding the yarn in front of the work.

STEP 3: Separate the knit and purl stitches by slipping the knit stitches onto one needle and the purl stitches onto a second needle, taking care not to twist the stitches during the transfer. Hold the two needles parallel with their business ends aligned and so that the knit stitches are on the front needle and the purl stitches are on the back needle.

STEP 4: Cut the yarn, leaving a tail at least three times the width to be bound off, and thread the tail on a tapestry needle.

STEP 5: Use a modification of the Kitchener stitch (see Glossary) to graft the two sets of stitches as follows:

1: Bring threaded tapestry needle from front to back (knitwise) through the first knit stitch on the front needle, pull the yarn through, and drop this stitch off the needle.

2: Bring the tapestry needle from back to front (purlwise) through the next knit stitch on the front needle, pull the yarn through, and leave this stitch on the needle.

3: Bring the tapestry needle from back to front (purlwise) through the first purl stitch on the back needle, pull the yarn through, and drop this stitch off the needle.

4: Bring the tapestry needle from front to back (knitwise) through the next purl stitch on the back needle, pull the yarn through, and leave this stitch on the needle.

Repeat these 4 steps until all stitches have been bound off.

Bianca
HEADBAND

Given my fondness for fine-gauge yarns, it's not often that I can complete a project in a single day. This headband is knitted with sportweight yarn, but its small size qualifies it for a "quick knit." You'll find that when knitting with this pure cashmere, you'll savor every last minimalistic stitch. For a more casual headband, use a hardy wool or cotton; for something slinky, use shimmery silk. In any case, the adjustable band fastened with buttons at the nape of the neck will allow you to slip on a little luxury in no time.

FINISHED SIZE

About 4" (10 cm) wide and 22½" (57 cm) long; wearing length is adjustable.

yarn

DK weight (#3 Light).

SHOWN HERE: Lion Brand LB Collection Cashmere (100% cashmere; 82 yd [75 m]/25 g): #124 toffee, 1 skein.

needles

U.S. size 5 (3.75 mm).

Adjust needle size if necessary to obtain the correct gauge.

notions

Stitch markers; cable needle (cn), tapestry needle; six ⅜" (1 cm) buttons.

gauge

24 sts and 32 rows = 4" (10 cm) in k3, p1 rib.

Stitch guide

3/4 LCP:

Sl 3 sts onto cable needle (cn) and hold in front, k3, p1, then k3 from cn.

3/4 RCP:

Sl 4 sts onto cn and hold in back, k3, then p1, k3 from cn.

Cabled Knot (panel of 25 sts)

ROWS 1, 5, 9, 13, AND 17: (RS) [P1, k3] 6 times, p1.

ROW 2 AND ALL WS ROWS: [K1, p3] 6 times, k1.

ROW 3: [P1, k3] 2 times, p1, 3/4RCP, [p1, k3] 2 times, p1.

ROWS 7 AND 15: P1, k3, p1, 3/4LCP, p1, 3/4LPC, p1, k3, p1.

ROW 11: [P1, 3/4RCP] 3 times, p1.

ROW 19: Rep Row 3.

ROW 20: [K1, p3] 6 times, k1.

Headband

CO 17 sts.

ROW 1: (RS) P1, k1, [p1, k2] 4 times, p1, k1, p1.

ROW 2: (WS) K1, p1, [k1, p2] 4 times, k1, p1, k1.

Rep these 2 rows until piece measures 3¼" (8.5 cm) from CO, ending with a WS row.

Increase to Taper

ROW 1: (RS) P1, M1 (see Glossary), k1, [p1, k2] 4 times, p1, k1, M1, p1—19 sts.

ROW 2: (WS) [K1, p2] 6 times, k1.

ROW 3: [P1, k2] 6 times, p1.

ROWS 4–6: Rep Rows 2 and 3 once, then work Row 2 once more.

ROW 7: P1, M1, k2, [p1, k2] 4 times, p1, k2, M1, p1—21 sts.

ROW 8: K1, p3, [k1, p2] 4 times, k1, p3, k1.

ROW 9: P1, k3, [p1, k2] 4 times, p1, k3, p1.

ROWS 10–12: Rep Rows 8 and 9 once, then work Row 8 once more.

ROW 13: P1, k3, p1, M1, k2, [p1, k2] 3 times, M1, p1, k3, p1—23 sts.

ROW 14: [K1, p3] 2 times, [k1, p2] 2 times, [k1, p3] 2 times, k1.

ROW 15: [P1, k3] 2 times, [p1, k2] 2 times, [p1, k3] 2 times, p1.

ROWS 16–18: Rep Rows 14 and 15 once, then work Row 14 once more.

ROW 19: [P1, k3] 2 times, p1, M1, k2, p1, k2, M1, [p1, k3] 2 times, p1—25 sts.

ROW 20: [K1, p3] 6 times, k1.

ROW 21: [P1, k3] 6 times, p1.

Rep Rows 20 and 21 (knit the knits and purl the purls) until piece measures 8¼" (21 cm) from CO, ending with a WS row.

Center

Work Rows 1–20 of cabled knot patt (see Stitch Guide) once—piece measures about 10½" (26.5 cm) from CO. Cont in k3, p1 rib as established until piece measures 16¼" (41.5 cm) from CO, ending with a WS row.

Decrease to Taper

ROW 1: (RS) [P1, k3] 2 times, p1, ssk, k1, p1, k1, k2tog, [p1, k3] 2 times, p1—23 sts rem.

ROW 2: [K1, p3] 2 times, [k1, p2] 2 times, [k1, p3] 2 times, k1.

ROW 3: [P1, k3] 2 times, [p1, k2] 2 times, [p1, k3] 2 times, p1.

ROWS 4–6: Rep Rows 2 and 3 once, then work Row 2 once more.

ROW 7: P1, k3, p1, ssk, k1, [p1, k2] 2 times, p1, k1, k2tog, p1, k3, p1—21 sts rem.

ROW 8: K1, p3, [k1, p2] 4 times, k1, p3, k1.

ROW 9: P1, k3, [p1, k2] 4 times, p1, k3, p1.

ROWS 10–12: Rep Rows 8 and 9 once, then work Row 8 once more.

ROW 13: P1, ssk, k1, [p1, k2] 4 times, p1, k1, k2tog, p1—19 sts rem.

ROW 14: [K1, p2] 6 times, k1.

ROW 15: [P1, k2] 6 times, p1.

Rep the last 2 rows until piece measures 20¼" (51.5 cm) from CO, ending with a WS row.

BUTTONHOLE ROW: (RS) Keeping rib patt as established, work first 4 sts, work one-row 2-st buttonhole (see Glossary), work in patt to last 6 sts, work 2-st buttonhole, work last 4 sts—2 buttonholes completed.

[Work 5 rows even in established rib, then rep the buttonhole row] 2 times—3 buttonhole rows total. Work even in patt until piece measures 22½" (57 cm) from CO, ending with a WS row. BO all sts in patt.

Finishing

Weave in loose ends. Block lightly.

Lap buttonhole end over plain end, try headband on, and pin the ends where best fit is achieved. Sew 6 buttons to RS of plain end, underneath buttonholes and with each button centered on a k2 column.

Ornati
GLOVES

Rows of vikkel braids across the cuffs, pearl-like buttons, and argyle motifs—composed of stacked twisted stitches—along the backs of the hands give a feminine feel to these decorative gloves. These gloves begin with the cuffs, which are worked flat; then stitches are picked up for the hands, which are worked in the round. The hands are best worked with the magic-loop method that allows knitting very small circumferences (like fingers) on circular needles. A fine-gauge yarn ensures that all the elements fit comfortably within the confines of this limited canvas.

FINISHED SIZE

About 7 (7½, 8)" (18 [19, 20.5] cm) hand circumference.

Gloves shown measure 7" (18 cm).

yarn
Fingering weight (#1 Super Fine).

SHOWN HERE: Cascade Yarns Heritage (75% superwash merino, 25% nylon; 437 yd [400 m]/100 g): #5632 purple, 1 skein for all sizes.

needles
Size U.S. 3 (3.25 mm): 40" (100 cm) circular (cir).

Adjust needle size if necessary to obtain the correct gauge.

notions
Markers (m; 3 different colors for beg of rnd, thumb gusset, and chart pattern); cable needle (cn); waste yarn stitch holders; tapestry needle; six ⅜" (1 cm) buttons.

gauge
30 sts and 43 rnds = 4" (10 cm) in St st worked in rnds.

NEXT RND: K26 (28, 30) palm sts, pm in gusset color, k1, pm in gusset color, k5 (6, 7), pm in chart color, work Rnd 1 of Argyle chart (page 41) over next 16 sts, pm in chart color, k5 (6, 7).

INC RND: Keeping in patt, work to gusset m, slip marker (sl m), M1, knit to next gusset m, M1, sl m, work in patt to end—2 gusset sts inc'd.

[Work 2 rnds even, then rep the inc rnd] 4 (5, 6) times—63 (69, 75) sts total; 11 (13, 15) sts between gusset markers. [Work 3 rnds even, then rep the inc rnd] 3 times—69 (75, 81) sts total; 17 (19, 21) sts between gusset markers; gusset measures 2½ (2¾, 3)" (6.5 [7, 7.5] cm) from joining rnd, measured straight up along a single column of sts; do not measure along diagonal shaping lines.

NOTE: When Rnd 33 of Argyle chart has been completed, remove m on each side of chart section and change to working the 16 chart sts in St st.

DIVIDING RND: Work to thumb gusset m, remove gusset m, place 17 (19, 21) thumb sts on waste yarn holder, remove second gusset m, use the backward-loop method (see Glossary) to CO 3 sts over thumb gap, work in patt to end—55 (59, 63) sts.

NEXT RND: Work to 1 st before newly CO sts, k2tog, k1, k2tog, work in patt to end—53 (57, 61) sts rem.

Work even as established until piece measures 3½ (3¾, 4¼)" (9 [9.5, 11] cm) from joining rnd.

Little Finger

K6 (7, 8), place next 42 (44, 46) sts on waste yarn holder, use the backward-loop method to CO 2 sts over gap for all sizes, k5 (6, 7)—13 (15, 17) sts. Work even in rnds until finger measures 2 (2¼, 2½)" (5 [5.5, 6.5] cm) or just below the tip of the wearer's little finger.

DEC RND: [K2tog] 5 (6, 7) times, k3tog—6 (7, 8) sts rem.

Cut yarn, leaving a 10" (25.5 cm) tail. Thread tail on a tapestry needle, draw through rem sts, pull tight to close hole, and fasten off on WS.

Left Glove

Cuff

CO 54 (58, 62) sts. Do not join. Work back and forth in rows as foll:

ROW 1: (RS) *Skip the first st on left-hand needle, knit the second st through the back loop (tbl) but leave this st on the left needle, knit the first st, then drop both sts off the left-hand needle; rep from *.

ROW 2: (WS) K1, purl to last st, k1.

ROW 3: (buttonhole row) Knit to last 4 sts, work [yo, k2tog] for buttonhole, k2.

ROWS 4–6: Work even in St st, beg and ending with a WS row.

ROWS 7–12: Rep Rows 1–6.

ROWS 13–17: Rep Rows 1–5, ending with a RS row.

ROW 18: (WS) BO 4 sts, purl to end—50 (54, 58) sts rem; cuff measures about 1¾" (4.5 cm) from CO.

Shape Thumb Gusset

JOINING RND: (RS) [K16, M1 (see Glossary)] 3 times, k2 (6, 10), place marker (pm) in color for beg of rnd, and join for working in rnds—53 (57, 61) sts; rnd begins at little finger side of the hand, at start of palm sts.

Upper Hand

Return 42 (44, 46) held sts to needle. With RS facing, join yarn at end of sts, next to little finger gap. Pick up and knit 2 (2, 3) sts from CO sts at base of little finger, knit to end, pm for beg of rnd—44 (46, 49) sts. Work even in the rnd for ¼ (¼, ½)" (6 mm [6 mm, 1.3 cm]).

Ring Finger

K8 (8, 9), place next 28 (30, 31) sts on waste yarn, use the backward-loop method to CO 2 (3, 3) sts over the gap, k8 (8, 9)—18 (19, 21) sts. Work even in rnds until finger measures 2¾ (3, 3¼)" (7 [7.5, 8.5] cm) or just below the tip of the wearer's ring finger.

DEC RND: [K2tog] 9 (8, 9) times, k3tog 0 (1, 1) time—9 (9, 10) sts rem.

Cut yarn, leaving a 10" (25.5 cm) tail. Thread tail on a tapestry needle, draw through rem sts, pull tight to close hole, and fasten off on WS.

Middle Finger

With RS facing, return first 7 (7, 8) held sts and last 7 held sts to needle—14 (16, 16) sts rem on holder. With RS facing, join yarn to end of first 7 (7, 8) finger sts, use the backward-loop method to CO 2 (3, 3) sts over gap, knit last 7 finger sts, then pick up and k2 (2, 3) sts from CO sts at base of ring finger—18 (19, 21) sts. Work even in rnds until finger measures 3 (3¼, 3½)" (7.5 [8.5, 9] cm) or just below the tip of the wearer's middle finger.

DEC RND: [K2tog] 9 (8, 9) times, k3tog 0 (1, 1) time—9 (9, 10) sts rem.

Cut yarn, leaving a 10" (25.5 cm) tail. Thread tail on a tapestry needle, draw through rem sts, pull tight to close hole, and fasten off on WS.

Index Finger

Return rem 14 (16, 16) held sts to needle. With RS facing, pick up and knit 3 (3, 4) sts from sts CO at base of middle finger, knit to end—17 (19, 20) sts. Work even in rnds until finger

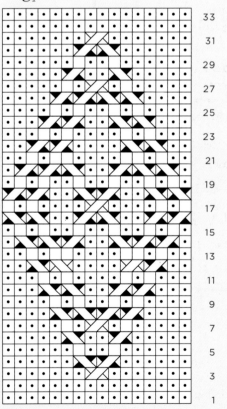

| knit |
| purl |

- ◻ knit
- ▫• purl
- ⬕ sl 1 st onto cn and hold in back, k1, p1 from cn
- ⬔ sl 1 st onto cn and hold in front, p1, k1 from cn
- ⬕ sl 1 st onto cn and hold in back, k1, k1 from cn
- ⬔ sl 1 st onto cn and hold in front, k1, k1 from cn

Argyle

measures 2¾ (3, 3¼)" (7 [7.5, 8.5] cm) or just below the tip of the wearer's index finger.

DEC RND: [K2tog] 7 (8, 10) times, k3tog 1 (1, 0) time—8 (9, 10) sts rem.

Cut yarn, leaving a 10" (25.5 cm) tail. Thread tail on a tapestry needle, draw through rem sts, pull tight to close hole, and fasten off on WS.

Thumb

Return 17 (19, 21) held thumb sts to needle, join yarn to beg of sts CO over thumb gap, pick up and knit 2 (2, 3) sts from base of sts CO over thumb gap—19 (21, 24) sts. Work even in rnds until thumb measures 2 (2¼, 2½)" (5 [5.5, 6.5] cm) or just below the tip of the wearer's thumb.

DEC RND: [K2tog] 8 (9, 12) times, k3tog 1 (1, 0) time—9 (10, 12) sts rem.

Cut yarn, leaving a 10" (25.5 cm) tail. Thread tail on a tapestry needle, draw through rem sts, pull tight to close hole, and fasten off on WS.

Right Glove
Cuff

CO 54 (58, 62) sts. Do not join. Work back and forth in rows as foll:

ROW 1: (RS) *Skip the first st on left-hand needle, knit the second st tbl but leave this st on the left needle, knit the first st, then drop both sts off the left-hand needle; rep from *.

ROW 2: (WS) K1, purl to last st, k1.

ROW 3: (buttonhole row) K2, work [yo, k2tog] for buttonhole, knit to end.

ROWS 4-6: Work even in St st, beg and ending with a WS row.

ROWS 7-18: Rep Rows 1-6 two more times, ending with a WS row.

NEXT ROW: (RS) BO 4 sts, knit to end—50 (54, 58) sts rem; cuff measures about 1¾" (4.5 cm) from CO.

Shape Thumb Gusset

JOINING RND: (RS) [K16, M1] 3 times, k2 (6, 10), pm in color for beg of rnd, and join for working in rnds—53 (57, 61) sts; rnd begins at little finger side of the hand, at start of back-of-hand sts.

NEXT RND: K5 (6, 7), pm in chart color, work Rnd 1 of Argyle chart over next 16 sts, pm in chart color, k5 (6, 7), pm in gusset color, k1, pm in gusset color, k26 (28, 30) palm sts.

Work as for right glove until gusset shaping has been completed—69 (75, 81) sts total; 17 (19, 21) sts between gusset markers; gusset measures 2½ (2¾, 3)" (6.5 [7, 7.5] cm) from joining rnd, measured straight up along a single column of sts.

NOTE: As for left glove, change to working chart sts in St st after chart Rnd 33 has been completed.

DIVIDING RND: Work to thumb gusset m, remove gusset m, place 17 (19, 21) thumb sts on waste yarn holder, remove second gusset m, use the backward-loop method to CO 3 sts over thumb gap, work in patt to end—55 (59, 63) sts.

NEXT RND: Work to 1 st before newly CO sts, k2tog, k1, k2tog, work in patt to end—53 (57, 61) sts rem.

Work even as established until piece measures 3½ (3¾, 4¼)" (9 [9.5, 11] cm) from joining rnd.

Little Finger and Upper Hand

Work as for left glove—44 (46, 49) sts rem; upper hand measures ¼ (¼, ½)" (6 mm [6 mm, 1.3 cm]) from sts picked up at base of little finger.

Ring, Middle, and Index Fingers

Work as for left glove—no hand sts rem.

Thumb

Work as for left glove.

Finishing

Weave in loose ends. Block lightly. Sew buttons to cuff, opposite buttonholes.

Magic-Loop Method

I love knitting with circular needles. I find them more portable than straight needles—they fit easily in almost any size bag or purse—and they put less strain on my wrists and arms when I'm knitting. When I first started knitting gloves and hats in the round, I relied on an assortment of knitting needles—longer ones for larger circumferences and shorter ones for intermediate circumferences, as well as double-pointed needles for the tiny fingers. But, as soon as a friend showed me the magic-loop method of knitting in the round, I was hooked. This method allows a single long circular needle to be used for any circumference. Theoretically, the length of the cable should be about three times longer than the circumference of the item you want to knit. A 40" (100 cm) length is most versatile, but a 32" (80 cm) length will work in a pinch.

STEP 1: Cast on the desired number of stitches on the long circular needle, then push all of the stitches onto the cable portion of the needle.

STEP 2: Locate the boundary between the two center stitches (or as close to the center as possible), then pull out a loop of cable from this point so that the stitches are divided between the two halves of the needle. Move each set of stitches to their respective needle tip and hold the two tips parallel so that the working yarn is attached to the first stitch of the back needle.

STEP 3: Pull out the tip of the back needle so that the stitches on that needle slide onto the cable, then bring this needle tip in position to work the first stitch of the group on the front needle—there will be two loops of cable; one between each group of stitches.

STEP 4: Use the back needle tip to work across all of the stitches on the front needle.

STEP 5: Rotate the work and arrange the stitches again so that the stitches just worked are on the back needle, the stitches yet to be worked are on the front needle, and the working yarn is attached to the first stitch on the back needle.

Repeat Steps 3–5 for the desired length.

Joining for Working in Rounds

To minimize gaps when joining the stitches for working in rounds, I like to cast on one extra stitch, then knit this extra stitch together with the first stitch of the first round. When working mittens or gloves, I also like to cast on an extra stitch on each side of the stitch(es) cast on over the gap formed when gusset stitches are placed on a holder. I then decrease these extra stitches on the next round by knitting them together with their neighbors. I do the same when working fingers on gloves—I cast on an extra stitch on each side of stitches picked up for each finger, then decrease these extra stitches on the following round. Doing so minimizes the holes at the bases of the fingers beautifully.

Avoiding Ladders of Loose Stitches

Whether you're working in the round with double-pointed needles or a long circular needle in the magic-loop method, there is a danger of a "ladder of loose stitches" forming at the boundary between needles. This column of loose stitches is caused by slight tension differences between the last stitch on one needle and the first stitch on the next needle. To minimize these differences, or eliminate them altogether, periodically shift the position of the boundaries between needles when working with double-pointed needles or shift the positions of the cable loops when using the magic-loop method.

Miele
HAT AND MITTENS

The simple hat-and-mitten set is elevated to the ranks of luxury when paired with an opulent alpaca/merino/bamboo yarn. I particularly like the contrast between the substantial k1, p1 ribbing worked with two strands of yarn held together and the airy openwork pattern worked with a single strand. To simplify the knitting and eliminate the need to incorporate decreases in the lace pattern, all of the shaping is worked in the ribbing. The yarn used here comes in a wide range of subtly rich colors—choose your favorite for the most elegant set you may ever own.

FINISHED SIZE

Mittens: About 7¼ (8¼)" (18.5 [21] cm) hand circumference, with option for adjusting length. Mittens shown measure 7¼" (18.5 cm).

Hat: About 19 (20¾, 22¾)" (48.5 [52.5, 58] cm) head circumference. Hat shown measures 19" (48.5 cm).

yarn

Fingering weight (#1 Super Fine).

SHOWN HERE: The Fibre Company Canopy Fingering (50% baby alpaca, 30% merino, 20% bamboo viscose; 200 yd [183 m]/50 g): blue quandons, 3 skeins for set in all sizes; 1 skein for mittens only in all sizes.

needles

MITTEN HANDS AND MAIN SECTION OF HAT: size U.S. 3 (3.25 mm): set of 4 or 5 double-pointed (dpn) or 40" circular (cir) for magic-loop method.

RIBBED CUFFS AND HAT BRIM: size U.S. 7 (4.5 mm): set of 4 or 5 dpn or 40" (100 cm) cir for magic-loop method.

Adjust needle size if necessary to obtain the correct gauge.

notions

Marker (m); waste yarn holders; tapestry needle.

gauge

26½ sts and 38 rows = 4" (10 cm) in hourglass pattern with a single strand of yarn on smaller needles.

22 sts and 28 rows = 4" (10 cm) in k1, p1 rib (slightly stretched) with yarn doubled on larger needles.

Stitch guide

Hourglass Pattern (multiple of 6 sts)

RNDS 1 AND 2: *K5, p1; rep from *.

RND 3: *Yo, ssk, p1, k2tog, yo, k1; rep from *.

RNDS 4, 5, AND 6: K2, *p1, k5; rep from * to last 4 sts, p1, k3.

RND 7: *K2tog, yo, k1, yo, ssk, p1; rep from *.

RND 8: *K5, p1; rep from *.

Rep Rnds 1–8 for pattern.

NOTES

» The right and left mittens are worked identically and can be worn on either hand.

» When working shaping in the hourglass pattern, if there are not enough stitches to work both a decrease and its companion yarnover, work the remaining stitch as k1 or p1 as necessary to maintain the hourglass pattern.

» Wear the hat with the ribbed gussets in the front and back (as shown) or with the ribbed gussets at the sides.

Hat

Brim

With larger needles and yarn doubled, use the tubular method (see Glossary) to CO 106 (118, 128) sts. Place marker (pm) and join for working in rnds, being careful not to twist sts. Work in k1, p1 rib until piece measures 2½" (6.5 cm) from CO. Change to smaller needles. Cut one strand and cont using single strand of yarn only.

Main Section

INC RND: K0 (11, 11), *M1 (see Glossary), k5; rep from * to last 6 (7, 7) sts, knit to end—126 (138, 150) sts.

Work in hourglass patt (see Stitch Guide) until piece measures 5¾" (14.5 cm) from CO and about 3¼" (8.5 cm) above last rnd of brim ribbing.

Ribbed Side Gussets

SET-UP RND: Work 36 (36, 42) sts in hourglass patt, *work first 2 sts of next patt rep (see Notes), pm, k2, [p1, k1] 10 (13, 13) times, p1, k2, pm, work last 3 sts of next patt rep,* work 30

(30, 36) sts in hourglass patt, rep from * to * once more—25 (31, 31) sts each in two new marked rib sections; each rib section beg and ends with k2.

Work 2 rnds even, working sts of ribbed side gussets between m as they appear (knit the knits, and purl the purls) and cont hourglass patt as established.

Shape Top

RND 1: *Work hourglass patt to m, slip marker (sl m), ssk, work in established rib patt to 2 sts before next m, k2tog, sl m; rep from * once more, work hourglass patt to end—4 sts dec'd; 2 sts dec'd from each side gusset.

RNDS 2-4: Work even in established patts.

Rep the last 4 rnds 4 more times—106 (118, 130) sts rem; 15 (21, 21) sts each side gusset. Rep Rnds 1 and 2 (i.e., dec every other rnd) 4 (6, 7) times—90 (94, 102) sts rem; 7 (9, 7) sts in each side gusset; ribbed section at top of hat measures about 3¼ (3½, 3¾)" (8.5 [9, 9.5] cm). Work even in patts as established until piece measures 9¾ (10¼, 10½)" (25 [26, 26.5] cm) from CO or desired finished length. Cut yarn, leaving a 24" (61 cm) tail to use for grafting top closed.

Finishing

Beg and ending as close as possible to the middle of a gusset section, place half of the sts on one strand of waste yarn and the other half of the sts on another strand of waste yarn—45 (47, 51) sts on each waste yarn holder. Block to measurements. Place each set of 45 (47, 51) sts on a separate needle. Turn the piece inside out so the right sides are touching and use the three-needle method (see Glossary) to BO the two sets of sts tog.

Weave in loose ends.

Mitten (make 2)
Cuff

With larger needles and two strands of yarn held together, use the tubular method (see Glossary) to CO 42 (48) sts. Place marker (pm) and join for working in rnds, being careful

not to twist sts. Work in k1, p1 rib until piece measures 2" (5 cm) from CO.

Change to smaller needles. Cut one strand and cont using single strand of yarn only.

Hand

INC RND: *M1 (see Glossary), k7 (8); rep from *—48 (54) sts.

RND 1: Work Rnd 1 of hourglass patt (see Stitch Guide) across all sts.

RND 2: Work 23 (26) sts in patt (see Notes), pm, work 1 st, pm, work rem 24 (27) sts in patt—1 st between gusset markers; rnd begins by little finger.

RNDS 3–5: Work in patt to first gusset m, slip marker (sl m), p1, sl m, work in patt to end—piece measures about 2½" (6.5 cm) from CO.

Shape Thumb Gusset

INC RND: Work in patt to first gusset m, sl m, M1, purl to second gusset m, M1, sl m, work in patt to end—2 sts inc'd inside gusset m.

NEXT RND: Work in patt to first gusset m, sl m, *k1, p1; rep from * to 1 st before second gusset m, k1, sl m, work in patt to end.

Rep the last 2 rnds 3 (4) more times, working inc'd gusset sts into established k1, p1 rib—56 (64) sts total; 9 (11) sts between gusset m. Work the inc rnd every 3 rnds 5 times, working inc'd sts into k1, p1 rib as established—66 (74) sts total; 19 (21) sts between gusset markers. Work even in patts as established until piece measures 2¾ (3¼)" (7 [8.5] cm) from first gusset inc rnd and about 5¼ (5¾)" (13.5 [14.5] cm) from CO.

NEXT RND: Work in patt to first gusset m, place 19 (21) thumb sts on waste yarn holder, work in patt to end—47 (53) sts rem.

NEXT RND: Work in patt to thumb gusset gap, use the backward-loop method (see Glossary) to CO 1 st over gap created by held gusset sts, work in patt to end—48 (54) sts. Work all sts even in hourglass patt as established until hand measures 5¾ (6¾)" (14.5 [17] cm) above last rnd of cuff ribbing or 1½ (2)" (3.8 [5] cm) less than length to tip of longest finger.

Shape Top

NEXT RND: *K1, p1; rep from *.

Dec mitten top for your size as foll:

Size 7¼" (18.5 cm) only

RND 1: *Sl 1, k2tog, psso, [p1, k1] 4 times, p1; rep from *—40 sts rem.

RNDS 2, 4, AND 6: *K1, p1; rep from *.

RND 3: *Sl 1, k2tog, psso, [p1, k1] 3 times, p1; rep from *—32 sts rem.

RND 5: *Sl 1, k2tog, psso, [p1, k1] 2 times, p1; rep from *—24 sts rem.

RND 7: *Sl 1, k2tog, psso, p1, k1, p1; rep from *—16 sts rem.

RNDS 8–10: *K1, p1; rep from *.

RND 11: *Sl 1, k2tog, psso, p1; rep from *—8 sts rem.

RNDS 12–14: *K1, p1; rep from *—after completing Rnd 14 ribbed section of mitten top measures 1½" (3.8 cm); hand measures about 7¼" (18.5 cm) above last rnd of cuff ribbing; piece measures 9¼" (23.5 cm) total from CO.

Size 8¼" (21 cm) only

RND 1: *Sl 1, k2tog, psso, [p1, k1] 3 times, pm, p3tog, [k1, p1] 3 times; rep from *—42 sts rem.

RNDS 2–4: *K1, p1; rep from *.

RND 5: *Sl 1, k2tog, psso, [p1, k1] 2 times, sl m, p3tog, [k1, p1] 2 times; rep from *—30 sts rem.

RNDS 6–9: *K1, p1; rep from *.

RND 10: *Sl 1, k2tog, psso, p1, k1, sl m, p3tog, k1, p1; rep from *—18 sts rem.

RNDS 11–14: *K1, p1; rep from *.

RND 15: *Sl 1, k2tog, psso, sl m, p3tog; rep from *—6 sts rem.

RNDS 16–19: *K1, p1; rep from*—after completing Rnd 19 ribbed section of mitten top measures 2″ (5 cm); hand measures about 8¾″ (22 cm) above last rnd of cuff ribbing; piece measures 10¾″ (27.5 cm) total from CO.

BOTH SIZES

If making a longer mitten, cont in k1, p1 rib as established until hand measures desired length. Cut yarn, leaving a 10″ (25.5 cm) tail. Thread tail on a tapestry needle, draw through rem sts, pull tight to close hole, and fasten off on WS.

Thumb

Place 19 (21) held thumb gusset sts on needles. Join a single strand of yarn, pick up and knit 1 st from base of st CO over thumb gap, pm, and join for working in rnds—20 (22) sts total.

Working picked-up st into established patt, work in k1, p1 rib until thumb measures 2 (2½)″ (5 [6.5] cm).

DEC RND: *K2tog; rep from *—10 (11) sts rem.

Cut yarn, leaving a 10″ (25.5 cm) tail. Thread tail on a tapestry needle, draw through rem sts, pull tight to close hole, and fasten off on WS.

Finishing

Weave in loose ends. Block lightly.

Starflower
HAT

The stitch pattern in this head-hugging hat, reminiscent of stars or flowers, has just the barest hint of eyelets to compensate for sculptural decreases. The pattern flows organically into ribbing at the top, where the crown decreases are a breeze to execute. A folded hem punctuated with picots provides warmth and substance, while adding a bit of feminine flair. Make the brim longer to pull over chilled ears or work more rounds of ribbing before beginning the crown decreases for a slouched, insouciant look.

FINISHED SIZE
About 18 (20, 22)" (45.5 [51, 56] cm) circumference.

Hat shown measures 20" (51 cm).

yarn
Sportweight (#2 Fine).

SHOWN HERE: The Fibre Company Road to China Light (65% alpaca, 15% silk, 10% camel, 10% cashmere; 159 yd [145 m]/50 g): jade, 2 skeins for all sizes.

needles
Size U.S. 3 (3.25 mm): set of 4 or 5 double-pointed (dpn) or 40" (100 cm) circular (cir) for working in magic-loop method.

Adjust needle size if necessary to obtain the correct gauge.

notions
Markers (m); tapestry needle.

gauge
24 sts and 46 rnds = 4" (10 cm) in lace patt worked in rounds.

23 sts and 40 rnds = 4" (10 cm) in St st worked in rounds.

stitch guide

Lace Pattern (multiple of 12 sts)

RND 1: *Yo, k2, ssk, k3, k2tog, k2, yo, k1; rep from *.

EVEN-NUMBERED RNDS 2–18: Knit.

RND 3: *K1, yo, k2, ssk, k1, k2tog, k2, yo, k2; rep from *.

RND 5: *K2, yo, k2, sl 1, k2tog, psso, k2, yo, k3; rep from *.

RND 7: *K2, yo, k5, yo, k2, sl 1, k2tog, psso; rep from *.

RND 9: *K2tog, k2, yo, k3, yo, k2, ssk, k1; rep from *.

RND 11: *K1, k2tog, k2, yo, k1, yo, k2, ssk, k2; rep from *.

RND 13: Rep Rnd 9.

RND 15: Rep Rnd 7.

RND 17: Rep Rnd 5.

RND 19: Rep Rnd 3.

RND 20: Knit.

Rep Rnds 1–20 for pattern.

Hat

CO 101 (113, 125) sts. Arrange sts on your choice of needle(s), place marker (pm), and join for working in rnds, being careful not to twist sts. Work even in St st (knit every rnd) until piece measures 1″ (2.5 cm) from CO.

NEXT RND: (picot fold line) K1, *yo, k2tog; rep from *.

Work even in St st until pieces measures 2″ (5 cm) from CO.

INC RND: *K14 (16, 17), M1 (see Glossary); rep from * to last 3 (1, 6) st(s), k3 (1, 6)—108 (120, 132) sts.

Work Rnds 1–20 of lace patt (see Stitch Guide), then work Rnds 1–9 once more—29 lace patt rnds total; piece measures about 4½″ (11.5 cm) from CO and 3½″ (9 cm) from picot fold line.

NEXT RND: K1, *p3, k3; rep from * to last 5 sts, p3, k2, remove end-of-rnd marker, knit the first st of the rnd again, replace marker—the marker has moved 1 st to the left; rnd now begins with p3 and ends with k3.

Cont in p3, k3 rib as established (knit the knits and purl the purls) until piece measures 6¾ (6¾, 7½)″ (17 [17, 19] cm) from picot fold line, or desired length.

Dec for crown as foll:

RND 1: *P2tog, p1, k3; rep from *—90 (100, 110) sts rem.

RNDS 3–5: *P2, k3; rep from *.

RND 6: *P2, k2tog, k1; rep from *—72 (80, 88) sts rem.

RNDS 7–9: *P2, k2; rep from *.

RND 10: *P2tog, k2; rep from *—54 (60, 66) sts rem.

RNDS 11 AND 12: *P1, k2; rep from *.

RND 13: *P1, k2tog; rep from *—36 (40, 44) sts rem.

RND 14: *P1, k1; rep from *.

RND 15: *K2tog; rep from *—18 (20, 22) sts rem; piece measures about 8¼ (8¼, 9)″ (21 [21, 23] cm) from picot fold line.

Finishing

Cut yarn, leaving a 10″ (25.5 cm) tail. Thread tail on a tapestry needle, draw through rem sts, pull tight to close hole, and fasten off on WS.

Weave in loose ends. Block lightly.

Gems
HOODIE

This knitted hoodie is elevated from its fleece brethren, yet retains the wearing ease of its humble roots. Worked in a sportweight merino that's tightly spun to resist pilling, this version embodies a duality of ease and elegance. Small rope cables travel up the center front edges and continue uninterrupted into the hood, while bubble-texture panels provide some interest to the front yoke. To minimize seaming, this hoodie is worked in one piece to the armholes, and the sleeves are worked in the round from the shoulders down to the cuffs.

FINISHED SIZE

About 32½ (36¼, 39¾, 43½, 47¾, 51½)" (82.5 [92, 101, 110.5, 121.5, 131] cm) bust circumference with fronts meeting at center.

Hoodie shown measures 36¼" (92 cm)

yarn
Sportweight (#2 Fine).

SHOWN HERE: Louet Gems Sport (100% merino; 225 yd [205 m]/100 g): #54 teal, 6 (6, 7, 7, 8, 8) skeins.

needles
Size U.S. 5 (3.75 mm): 24" (60 cm) circular (cir) and set of 4 or 5 double-pointed (dpn).

Adjust needle size if necessary to obtain the correct gauge.

notions
Markers (m); stitch holders; spare needle in same size as main needle for three-needle bind-off; tapestry needle.

gauge
22 sts and 30 rows = 4" (10 cm) in St st.

22 (32) sts from Rows 1, 2, 25, and 26 of Right and Left Bubble Panels measure 4 (5¾)" (10 [14.5] cm) wide (see Notes).

9 sts of each front band (3 I-cord edging sts, 2 rev St sts, and 4 rope cable sts) measure 1" (2.5 cm) wide.

Stitch guide

Rope Cable (worked over 4 sts)

ROW 1: (RS) K4.

ROW 2: (WS) P4.

ROW 3: Sl 2 sts onto cable needle (cn) and hold in back of work, k2, k2 from cn.

ROW 4: P4.

Rep Rows 1–4 for pattern.

I-cord Edging (worked over 3 sts)

ROW 1: (RS) K1, sl 1 purlwise with yarn in front (pwise wyf), k1.

ROW 2: (WS) Sl 1 pwise wyf, k1, sl 1 pwise wyf.

Rep Rows 1 and 2 for pattern.

NOTES

» Because the stitch counts of the Bubble charts do not remain constant, the charts contain gray "no stitch" boxes that act as placeholders where stitches have been decreased away or where stitches will be added later. Skip over each "no stitch" symbol as you come to it; simply proceed to the next stitch.

» Each chart represents 22 to 26 stitches for the four smallest sizes and 32 to 36 stitches for the two largest sizes. For the four smallest sizes, ignore the yellow shaded section at the side of each chart and work only the stitches indicated for your size. For the two largest sizes, work across all stitches of the entire chart.

» Each bubble panel is 50 rows long. Work Rows 1–10 of each chart once, work Rows 11–18 four times, then work Rows 19–26 once. After completing Row 26, remove the panel marker and work the panel stitches in stockinette.

» When checking stitch counts during front shaping, count each bubble panel as 22 or 32 stitches, depending on your size (the same as the number of stockinette stitches above and below the panel), even if the chart happens to be on a row where the stitch count has temporarily increased.

» Give the I-cord edges a good tug vertically every now and then to stretch them to the same length as the main fabric. This will cause the middle stitch to recede between the two flanking stitches.

Body

With cir needle, CO 186 (206, 226, 246, 270, 290) sts. Do not join.

SET-UP ROW: (RS) Work Row 1 of I-cord edging (see Stitch Guide) over first 3 sts, [p2, k4] 7 (8, 9, 10, 11, 11) times, p2 (2, 1, 0, 0, 2), k1 (0, 0, 0, 0, 3), place marker (pm) for seam, sl 1 purlwise with yarn in back (pwise wyb), pm, k1 (0, 2, 1, 1, 0), [p2, k4] 14 (16, 17, 19, 21, 23) times, p2, k1 (0, 2, 1, 1, 0), pm for seam, sl 1 pwise wyb, pm, k1 (0, 0, 0, 0, 3), p2 (2, 1, 0, 0, 2), [k4, p2] 7 (8, 9, 10, 11, 11) times, work Row 1 of I-cord edging

over last 3 sts—48 (53, 58, 63, 69, 74) sts each front, 88 (98, 108, 118, 130, 140) back sts, 1 "seam" st at each side.

NOTE: Work the marked seam sts as sl 1 pwise wyb on RS rows and as p1 on WS rows, and slip the markers (sl m) on each side of the seam sts every row.

Keeping the first 3 and last 3 sts in I-cord edging and working seam sts as noted, work rem sts in established rib until piece measures 2¾" (7 cm) from CO, ending with WS row.

NEXT ROW: (RS) Work 3 sts I-cord edging, p2 for rev St st, work Row 1 of Rope Cable (see Stitch Guide) over 4 sts, pm

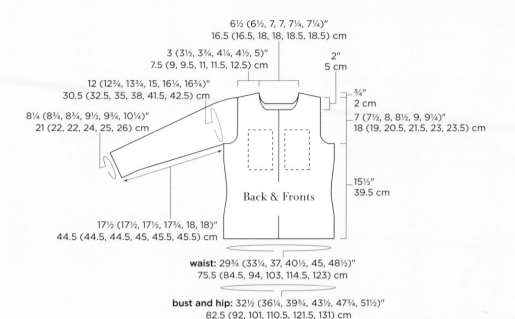

6½ (6½, 7, 7, 7¼, 7¼)"
16.5 (16.5, 18, 18, 18.5, 18.5) cm

3 (3½, 3¾, 4¼, 4½, 5)"
7.5 (9, 9.5, 11, 11.5, 12.5) cm

2"
5 cm

12 (12¾, 13¾, 15, 16¼, 16¾)"
30.5 (32.5, 35, 38, 41.5, 42.5) cm

¾"
2 cm

8¼ (8¾, 8¾, 9½, 9¾, 10¼)"
21 (22, 22, 24, 25, 26) cm

7 (7½, 8, 8½, 9, 9¼)"
18 (19, 20.5, 21.5, 23, 23.5) cm

15½"
39.5 cm

Back & Fronts

17½ (17½, 17½, 17¾, 18, 18)"
44.5 (44.5, 44.5, 45, 45.5, 45.5) cm

waist: 29¾ (33¼, 37, 40½, 45, 48½)"
75.5 (84.5, 94, 103, 114.5, 123) cm

bust and hip: 32½ (36¼, 39¾, 43½, 47¾, 51½)"
82.5 (92, 101, 110.5, 121.5, 131) cm

for end of right front band, knit to last 9 sts slipping seam sts as established, pm for beg of left front band, work Row 1 of Rope Cable over 4 sts, p2 for rev St st, work 3 sts I-cord edging.

Working seam st and 9 band sts at each front edge in established patts, work rem sts in St st until piece measures 3¾" (9.5 cm) from CO, ending with WS row.

DEC ROW: (RS) Keeping patts as established, *work to 3 sts before seam m, k2tog, k1, sl m, sl 1 pwise wyb (seam st), sl m, k1, ssk; rep from * once more, work in patt to end—4 sts dec'd.

[Work 7 rows even, then rep the dec row] 3 times—170 (190, 210, 230, 254, 274) sts rem. Work even until piece measures 8½" (21.5 cm) from CO, ending with a WS row.

NOTE: The Bubble Panel charts will be introduced while the waist increases are in progress; read all the way through the following sections before proceeding so you do not accidentally work past the point where the charts should begin.

INC ROW: (RS) Keeping patts as established, *work to 1 st before seam m, M1 (see Glossary), k1, sl m, sl 1 pwise wyb (seam st), sl m, k1, M1; rep from * once more, work in patt to end—4 sts inc'd.

[Work 9 rows even, then rep the inc row] 3 times—186 (206, 226, 246, 270, 290) sts (see Notes for how to account for Bubble Panel sts).

At the same time when piece measures 11¼" (28.5 cm) from CO, establish chart patts on next RS row as foll:

SET-UP ROW: (RS) Work 9 front band sts, sl m, work Row 1 of Right Bubble Panel chart over 22 (22, 22, 22, 32, 32) sts, pm, work in patt to last 31 (31, 31, 31, 41, 41) sts, including any waist incs if required for this row, pm, work Row 1 of Left Bubble Panel chart over 22 (22, 22, 22, 32, 32) sts, sl m, work 9 front band sts.

Cont in patts as established until piece measures 15½" (39.5 cm) from CO, ending with a WS row.

Left Bubble Panel

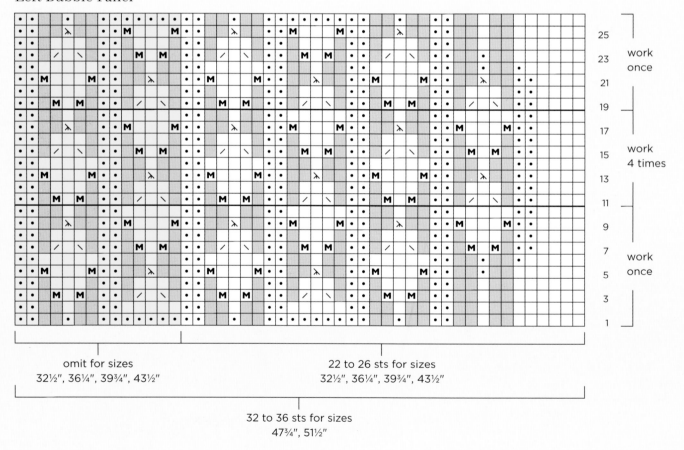

work once

work 4 times

work once

25

23

21

19

17

15

13

11

9

7

5

3

1

omit for sizes
32½", 36¼", 39¾", 43½"

22 to 26 sts for sizes
32½", 36¼", 39¾", 43½"

32 to 36 sts for sizes
47¾", 51½"

☐ knit on RS; purl on WS	╱ k2tog	M M1 (see Glossary)
· purl on RS; knit on WS	╲ ssk	⅄ sl 2, k1, p2sso
		▨ no stitch (see Notes)

Right Bubble Panel

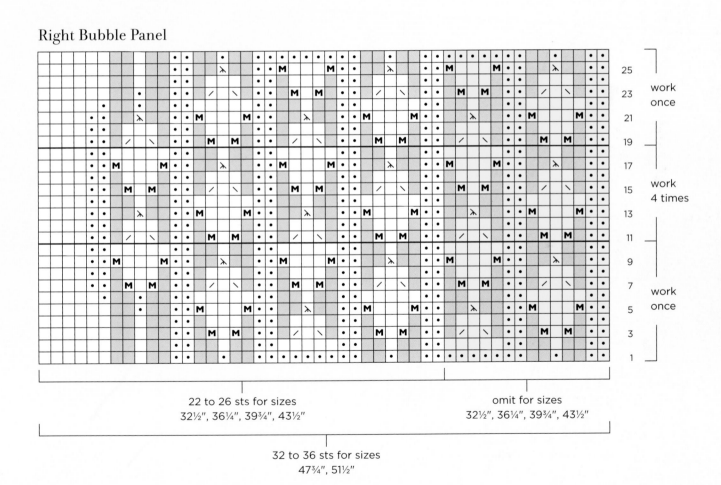

22 to 26 sts for sizes
32½", 36¼", 39¾", 43½"

omit for sizes
32½", 36¼", 39¾", 43½"

32 to 36 sts for sizes
47¾", 51½"

Divide for Fronts and Back

NEXT ROW: (RS) Keeping in patts, work 48 (53, 58, 63, 69, 74) right front sts, sl m, k1 (seam st), BO 5 (5, 7, 8, 10, 10) sts for right underarm, knit to m before next seam st, turn work—48 (53, 58, 63, 69, 74) right front sts and 1 seam st before BO gap; 83 (93, 101, 110, 120, 130) back sts; 1 seam st and 48 (53, 58, 63, 69, 74) left front sts rem unworked at end of needle.

Place sts for each front on separate holders or allow them to rest on needle while working the back sts.

Back

Work back and forth in rows on 83 (93, 101, 110, 120, 130) back sts only as foll:

NEXT ROW: (WS) BO 5 (5, 7, 8, 10, 10) sts, purl to end—78 (88, 94, 102, 110, 120) sts rem.

DEC ROW: (RS) K1, ssk, knit to last 3 sts, k2tog, k1—2 sts dec'd.

[Work 1 WS row even, then rep the dec row] 4 (5, 6, 7, 9, 12) times—68 (76, 80, 86, 90, 94) sts rem. Work even in St st until armholes measure 6 (6½, 7, 7½, 8, 8¼)" (15 [16.5, 18, 19, 20.5, 21] cm), ending with a WS row.

Shape Neck and Shoulders

NEXT ROW: (RS) K18 (22, 23, 26, 27, 29), BO center 32 (32, 34, 34, 36, 36) sts, knit to end—18 (22, 23, 26, 27, 29) sts rem each side.

Place sts for right neck and shoulder on holder or allow them to rest on needle while working the left neck and shoulder.

Left Side

Working on 18 (22, 23, 26, 27, 29) sts of left shoulder only, purl 1 WS row.

DEC ROW: (RS) K1, ssk, knit to end—1 st dec'd.

Rep the last 2 rows once more—16 (20, 21, 24, 25, 27) sts rem. Work even until armhole measures 7 (7½, 8, 8½, 9, 9¼)" (18 [19, 20.5, 21.5, 23, 23.5] cm), ending with a WS row. Shape shoulder with short-rows (see Glossary) as foll:

SHORT-ROW 1: (RS) Knit to last 5 (6, 7, 8, 8, 9) sts, wrap next st, turn work.

SHORT-ROWS 2 AND 4: (WS) Purl to end.

SHORT-ROW 3: Knit to last 10 (12, 14, 16, 16, 18) sts, wrap next st, turn.

NEXT ROW: (RS) Knit across all sts, working wraps tog with wrapped sts.

Place sts on holder.

Right Side

Return 18 (22, 23, 26, 27, 29) held right neck and shoulder sts to needle, if they are not already on the needle, and rejoin yarn with WS facing at neck edge. Purl 1 WS row.

DEC ROW: (RS) Knit to last 3 sts, k2tog, k1—1 st dec'd.

Rep the last 2 rows once more—16 (20, 21, 24, 25, 27) sts rem. Work even until armhole measures 7 (7½, 8, 8½, 9, 9¼)" (18 [19, 20.5, 21.5, 23, 23.5] cm), ending with a RS row. Shape shoulders with short-rows as foll:

SHORT-ROW 1: (WS) Purl to last 5 (6, 7, 8, 8, 9) sts, wrap next st, turn.

SHORT-ROWS 2 AND 4: (RS) Knit to end.

SHORT-ROW 3: Purl to last 10 (12, 14, 16, 16, 18) sts, wrap next st, turn.

NEXT ROW: (WS) Purl across all sts, working wraps tog with wrapped sts.

Place sts on holder.

Left Front

Return 48 (53, 58, 63, 69, 74) held left front sts and 1 seam st next to them to needle, if they are not already on the needle, and rejoin yarn with RS facing at armhole edge—49 (54, 59, 64, 70, 75) sts total.

NEXT ROW: (RS) BO 5 (5, 7, 8, 10, 10) sts, work in patt to end—44 (49, 52, 56, 60, 65) sts rem.

Work 1 WS row even.

DEC ROW: (RS) K1, ssk, work to end—1 st dec'd.

Rep the last 2 rows 4 (5, 6, 7, 9, 12) more times—39 (43, 45, 48, 50, 52) sts rem. Converting Bubble Panel sts to St st after Row 26 of chart has been completed, work even until armhole measures 5 (5½, 6, 6½, 7, 7¼)" (12.5 [14, 15, 16.5, 18, 18.5] cm), ending with a RS row.

Shape Neck and Shoulder

ROW 1: (WS) Keeping in patts as established, work 9 front band sts and place these sts on holder to be worked later for front edge of hood, BO 6 (6, 7, 7, 8, 8) sts, purl to end—24 (28, 29, 32, 33, 35) sts rem.

Make a note of the WS Rope Cable row just completed so you can resume the patt with the correct RS row for the hood. BO 3 sts at beg of next WS row, then BO 2 sts at beg of foll WS row—19 (23, 24, 27, 28, 30) sts rem.

DEC ROW: (RS) Knit to last 3 sts, k2tog, k1—1 st dec'd

[Work 1 WS row even, then rep the dec row] 2 times—16 (20, 21, 24, 25, 27) sts rem. Work even until armhole measures 7 (7½, 8, 8½, 9, 9¼)" (18 [19, 20.5, 21.5, 23, 23.5] cm), ending with a RS row. Shape shoulder using short-rows as for right back shoulder. Place sts on holder.

Right Front

Return 48 (53, 58, 63, 69, 74) held right front sts and 1 seam st next to them to needle, if they are not already on the needle, and rejoin yarn with WS facing at armhole edge—49 (54, 59, 64, 70, 75) sts total.

NEXT ROW: (WS) BO 5 (5, 7, 8, 10, 10) sts, work in patt to end—44 (49, 52, 56, 60, 65) sts rem.

DEC ROW: (RS) Work in patt to last 3 sts, k2tog, k1—1 st dec'd.

Work 1 WS row even. Rep the last 2 rows 4 (5, 6, 7, 9, 12) more times—39 (43, 45, 48, 50, 52) sts rem. Converting Bubble Panel sts to St st after Row 26 of chart has been completed, work even until armhole measures 5 (5½, 6, 6½, 7, 7¼)" (12.5 [14, 15, 16.5, 18, 18.5] cm), ending with a WS row.

Shape Neck and Shoulder

Break yarn and place 9 front band sts on holder—30 (34, 36, 39, 41, 43) sts rem. Make a note of the last WS Rope Cable row completed so you can resume the patt with the correct RS row for the hood. Rejoin yarn with RS facing to neck edge.

ROW 1: (RS) Keeping in patts as established, BO 6 (6, 7, 7, 8, 8) sts, knit to end—24 (28, 29, 32, 33, 35) sts rem.

BO 3 sts at beg of next RS row, then BO 2 sts at beg of foll RS row—19 (23, 24, 27, 28, 30) sts rem. Work 1 WS row even.

DEC ROW: (RS) K1, ssk, knit to end—1 st dec'd

[Work 1 WS row even, then rep the dec row] 2 times—16 (20, 21, 24, 25, 27) sts rem. Work even until armhole measures 7 (7½, 8, 8½, 9, 9¼)" (18 [19, 20.5, 21.5, 23, 23.5] cm), ending with a WS row. Shape shoulder using short-rows as for left back shoulder. Place sts on holder.

Join Shoulders

Block body to measurements. With RS touching and WS facing outward, use the three-needle method (see Glossary) to BO the 16 (20, 21, 24, 25, 27) front and back shoulder sts tog at each side.

Sleeves

With cir needle, RS facing, and beg at shoulder join, pick up and knit 28 (30, 31, 33, 35, 36) sts evenly spaced along armhole edge to beg of underarm BO (about 1 st for every 2 rows), pm, pick up and knit 10 (10, 14, 16, 20, 20) sts across underarm BO, pm, then 28 (30, 31, 33, 35, 36) sts evenly spaced along rem armhole edge to end at shoulder join, pm—66 (70, 76, 82, 90, 92) sts total.

Sleeves Worked from the Top Down

I often choose to knit sleeves—even set-in sleeves—in the round from the top down. In addition to eliminating the need for seams, this allows me to try on a sleeve and make length decisions along the way. The method I use is adapted from that provided in Barbara Walker's *Knitting from the Top* and Wendy Bernard's *Custom Knits*.

When knitting a set-in sleeve in pieces from the bottom up, the sleeve cap has a curved bell shape with a perimeter roughly equal that of the armhole of the body. The bound-off wings at the base of the cap match the initial bind off worked in the armhole shaping. The cap then follows the shape of the armhole, achieved with a faster rate of decreases at the beginning and end of the cap and a slower rate in the middle. The top of the cap is flat.

When worked from the top down, the same shape is achieved through a series of shorts-rows rather than decreases and bind-offs. To begin, pick up and knit stitches around the armhole opening, starting at the shoulder join and working down to the underarm, then back up the other side to end at the shoulder join. In general, pick up about one stitch for every two rows along vertical edges and pick up one stitch for every bound-off stitch across the base of the armhole. The cap is then shaped while working back and forth in short-rows. To begin, knit several stitches past the shoulder seam, wrap the next stitch, turn the work, and work back to several stitches past the shoulder seam on the other side. Then wrap the next stitch, turn the work, and work back in the other direction. Continue working back and forth in the manner, working more stitches each short-row until all stitches have been worked. In general, several stitches are worked past turning points at the top of the cap to produce a shallow angle (formed by working more decreases over fewer rows when working in pieces), then just one stitch is worked past turning points to produce the steeper angle (formed by working fewer decreases over more rows when working in pieces) toward the base of the cap. At the base of the cap, all of the stitches picked up across the bound-off edge of the armhole are knitted at once and the rest of the sleeve is worked in the round to the cuff.

Sleeve Cap

Work short-rows to shape cap as foll:

SHORT-ROW 1: (RS) K5, wrap next st, turn.

SHORT-ROW 2: (WS) Purl to shoulder join m, sl m, p5, wrap next st, turn.

SHORT-ROW 3: K5, sl m, k9 working wrap tog with wrapped st, wrap next st, turn.

SHORT-ROW 4: P9, sl m, p9 working wrap tog with wrapped st, wrap next st, turn.

SHORT-ROW 5: K9, sl m, k12 working wrap tog with wrapped st, wrap next st, turn.

SHORT-ROW 6: P12, sl m, p12 working wrap tog with wrapped st, wrap next st, turn.

SHORT-ROW 7: K12, sl m, k13 working wrap tog with wrapped st, wrap next st, turn.

SHORT-ROW 8: P13, sl m, p13 working wrap tog with wrapped st, wrap next st, turn—last wrapped st at each side is the 14th st from shoulder join m.

SHORT-ROW 9: Sl m as you come to it, knit to previously wrapped st, work wrap tog with wrapped st, wrap next st, turn—wrapped st is 1 st farther from shoulder join m.

SHORT-ROW 10: Sl m as you come to it, purl to previously wrapped st, work wrap tog with wrapped st, wrap next st, turn—wrapped st is 1 st farther from shoulder join m.

Rep the last 2 rows 13 (15, 16, 18, 20, 21) more times—last wrapped st at each side is the st next to m on each side of underarm sts.

NEXT ROW: (RS) Knit to shoulder m, remove m, knit to wrapped st, work wrap tog with wrapped st, remove m, k5 (5, 7, 8, 10, 10) to center of underarm, pm for center of underarm.

NEXT RND: Change to dpn. With RS still facing, knit 1 rnd on all sts, working wrap tog with wrapped st, and ending at underarm m—sleeve cap measures 5 (5½, 5¾, 6½, 7, 7¼)" (12.5 [14, 14.5, 16.5, 18, 18.5] cm) from pick-up row, measured straight up along a single column of sts in center of cap.

Lower Sleeve

Knit 3 rnds.

DEC RND: K1, ssk, knit to last 3 sts, k2tog, k1—2 sts dec'd.

Cont in St st, rep the dec rnd every 6th rnd 0 (0, 0, 0, 12, 13) times, then every 7th rnd 0 (0, 0, 6, 5, 4) times, then every 8th rnd 0 (0, 13, 8, 0, 0) times, then every 10th rnd 9 (10, 0, 0, 0, 0) times—46 (48, 48, 52, 54, 56) sts rem. Work even until sleeve measures 14½ (14½, 14½, 14¾, 15, 15)" (37 [37, 37, 37.5, 38, 38] cm) from joining rnd.

NEXT RND: *P2, k4; rep from * to last 4 (0, 0, 4, 0, 2) sts, p2 (0, 0, 2, 0, 2), k2 (0, 0, 2, 0, 0).

Work rib patt as established for 3" (7.5 cm)—sleeve measures 17½ (17½, 17½, 17¾, 18, 18)" (44.5 [44.5, 44.5, 45, 45.5, 45.5] cm) from joining rnd. Loosely BO all sts.

Finishing

Block lightly to measurements. Weave in loose ends.

Hood

With RS facing, join yarn to right front neck edge. Work 9 held right front band sts in established patt, then pick up and knit 23 (23, 24, 24, 25, 25) sts evenly spaced along right front neck, 42 sts across back neck (for all sizes), and 23 (23, 24, 24, 25, 25) sts along left front neck, then work 9 held left front band sts in established patt—106 (106, 108, 108, 110, 110) sts total. Maintaining band sts as established, work rem sts in St st until piece measures 2″ (5 cm) from pick-up row, ending with a RS row.

NEXT ROW: (WS) Keeping in patt as established, work 53 (53, 54, 54, 55, 55) sts, pm in center of hood, work to end.

INC ROW: (RS) Work to 5 sts before m, M1, k5, sl m, k5, M1, work to end—2 sts inc'd.

[Work 5 rows even, then rep the inc row] 6 times—120 (120, 122, 122, 124, 124) sts. Work even until piece measures 12 (12, 12½, 12½, 12¾, 12¾)″ (30.5 [30.5, 31.5, 31.5, 32.5, 32.5] cm) from pick-up row, ending with a WS row.

Left Hood Top

NEXT ROW: (RS) Keeping in patt, work 60 (60, 61, 61, 62, 62) sts for right hood, place sts just worked on holder to work later, work in patt to end—60 (60, 61, 61, 62, 62) left hood sts rem. Work short-rows as foll:

SHORT-ROW 1: (WS) Work to last 11 (11, 12, 12, 13, 13) sts, wrap next st, turn.

SHORT-ROWS 2, 4, AND 6: (RS) Work in patt to end.

SHORT-ROW 3: Work to last 15 (15, 16, 16, 17, 17) sts, wrap next st, turn.

SHORT-ROW 5: Work to last 20 (20, 21, 21, 22, 22) sts, wrap next st, turn.

SHORT-ROW 7: Work to last 27 (27, 28, 28, 29, 29) sts, wrap next st, turn.

SHORT-ROW 8: Work to end.

NEXT ROW: (WS) Work across all sts, working wraps tog with wrapped sts—piece measures 13¼ (13¼, 13¾, 13¾, 14, 14)″ (33.5 [33.5, 35, 35, 35.5, 35.5] cm) from pick-up row at front edge. Place sts on holder.

Right Hood Top

Return 60 (60, 61, 61, 62, 62) held right hood sts to needle and join yarn with WS facing in center of hood. Work 1 WS row even. Work short-rows as foll:

SHORT-ROW 1: (RS) Work in patt to last 11 (11, 12, 12, 13, 13) sts, wrap next st, turn.

SHORT-ROWS 2, 4, AND 6: (WS) Work to end.

SHORT-ROW 3: Work in patt to last 15 (15, 16, 16, 17, 17) sts, wrap next st, turn.

SHORT-ROW 5: Work in patt to last 20 (20, 21, 21, 22, 22) sts, wrap next st, turn.

SHORT-ROW 7: Work in patt to last 27 (27, 28, 28, 29, 29) sts, wrap next st, turn.

SHORT-ROW 8: Work to end.

NEXT ROW: (RS) Work across all sts, working wraps tog with wrapped sts—piece measures 13¼ (13¼, 13¾, 13¾, 14, 14)″ (33.5 [33.5, 35, 35, 35.5, 35.5] cm) from pick-up row at front edge. Leave sts on needle.

Join Top of Hood

Place 60 (60, 61, 61, 62, 62) held left hood sts on spare needle. Fold hood in half with RS touching and WS facing outward, use the three-needle method to BO the sts tog.

Weave in loose ends.

Honeycomb
TUNIC

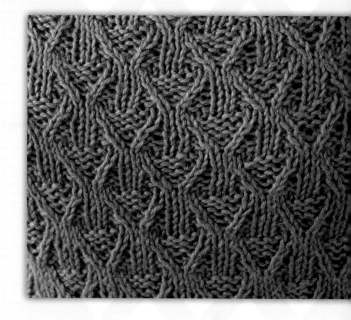

This body-hugging tunic is great for those days when you want a little warmth without a lot of bulk. Wear it as a long top over jeans or as a short dress over colorful tights. A generous portion of wickerwork pattern separates the sculptural ribs at the waist and neck. The lower edge is hemmed to provide a polished finish and a bit of weight to the skirt, whereas the neck and armholes are left clean and raw. Gentle shaping throughout ensures that the tunic follows your curves from top to bottom.

FINISHED SIZE

About 32 (34, 38, 42, 46, 51)" (81.5 [86.5, 96.5, 106.5, 117, 129.5] cm) bust circumference.

Tunic shown measures 34" (86.5 cm).

yarn
DK weight (#3 Light).

SHOWN HERE: Classic Elite Yarns Soft Linen (35% linen, 35% wool, 30% baby alpaca; 137 yd [125 m]/50 g): #2206 thistle (pink), 6 (6, 7, 8, 8, 9) skeins.

needles
BODY: size U.S. 6 (4 mm): 24" (60 cm) circular (cir).

HEM: size U.S. 5 (3.75 mm): 24" (60 cm) cir.

Adjust needle size if necessary to obtain the correct gauge.

notions
Waste yarn for provisional cast-on; spare cir needle same size or smaller than hem needle for joining hem; markers (m); cable needle (cn); stitch holders; tapestry needle.

gauge
22 sts and 32 rows = 4" in St st and wickerwork pattern on larger needles.

stitch guide

LT:

Sl 1 st onto cable needle (cn) and hold in front, k1, k1 from cn.

RT:

Sl 1 st onto cn and hold in back, k1, k1 from cn.

Wickerwork Pattern (multiple of 8 sts)

SET-UP ROW: (WS) P1, *k2, p2; rep from * to last 3 sts, k2, p1.

ROW 1: (RS) *K1, p1, RT, LT, p1, k1; rep from *.

ROW 2: *P1, k1, p1, k2, p1, k1, p1; rep from *.

ROW 3: *K1, RT, p2, LT, k1; rep from *

ROW 4: P2, *k4, p4; rep from * to last 6 sts, k4, p2.

ROW 5: Knit.

ROW 6: P1, *k2, p2; rep from * to last 3 sts, k2, p1.

ROW 7: *LT, p1, k2, p1, RT; rep from *.

ROW 8: *K1, p1, k1, p2, k1, p1, k1; rep from *.

ROW 9: *P1, LT, k2, RT, p1; rep from *.

ROW 10: K2, *p4, k4; rep from * to last 6 sts, p4, k2.

ROW 11: Knit.

ROW 12: Rep Row 6.

Rep Rows 1–12 for pattern.

NOTES

» During shaping, if there are not enough wickerwork pattern stitches to work a complete 2-stitch LT or RT, work the unpaired cable stitch in stockinette instead.

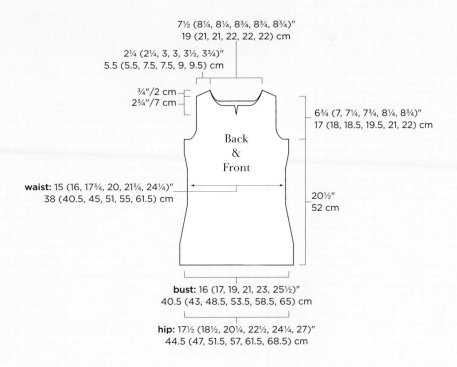

7½ (8¼, 8¼, 8¾, 8¾, 8¾)"
19 (21, 21, 22, 22, 22) cm

2¼ (2¼, 3, 3, 3½, 3¾)"
5.5 (5.5, 7.5, 7.5, 9, 9.5) cm

¾"/2 cm
2¾"/7 cm

6¾ (7, 7¼, 7¾, 8¼, 8¾)"
17 (18, 18.5, 19.5, 21, 22) cm

Back
&
Front

waist: 15 (16, 17¾, 20, 21¾, 24¼)"
38 (40.5, 45, 51, 55, 61.5) cm

20½"
52 cm

bust: 16 (17, 19, 21, 23, 25½)"
40.5 (43, 48.5, 53.5, 58.5, 65) cm

hip: 17½ (18½, 20¼, 22½, 24¼, 27)"
44.5 (47, 51.5, 57, 61.5, 68.5) cm

Back

With waste yarn, smaller cir needle, and using a provisional method (see Glossary), CO 96 (102, 112, 124, 134, 148) sts. Work 6 rows even in St st (knit RS rows; purl WS rows), ending with a WS row. Carefully remove the waste yarn from the provisional CO and place 96 (102, 112, 124, 134, 148) sts from base of CO on spare cir needle. Fold piece in half to bring needles tog with WS touching and RS facing out and with needle holding sts from base of CO in back.

JOINING ROW: (RS) *K2tog (1 st from each needle); rep from * until all hem sts have been joined—still 96 (102, 112, 124, 134, 148) sts; finished hem measures about ½" (1.3 cm) from fold line.

Change to larger cir needle. Work even in St st until piece measures 3½" (9 cm) from CO, ending with a RS row.

NEXT ROW: (WS) P21 (22, 24, 27, 29, 32), place marker (pm) for dart, p54 (58, 64, 70, 76, 84) center sts, pm for dart, purl to end.

DEC ROW: (RS) Knit to dart m, slip marker (sl m), ssk, knit to 2 sts before next m, k2tog, sl m, knit to end—2 sts dec'd.

[Work 7 rows even, then rep the dec row] 6 times—82 (88, 98, 110, 120, 134) sts. Purl 1 WS row, removing dart markers—piece measures 9¾" (25 cm) from hem fold line. Work ribbed waist section as foll:

NEXT ROW: (RS) K2 (1, 2, 0, 1, 0), *p2, k2; rep from * to last 4 (3, 4, 2, 3, 2) sts, p2, k2 (1, 2, 0, 1, 0).

Work sts as they appear (knit the knits and purl the purls) until rib section measures 3½" (9 cm) and piece measures 13¼" (33.5 cm) from hem fold line, ending with a RS row. Establish wickerwork patt (see Stitch Guide) as foll:

SET-UP ROW: (WS) K1 (0, 1, 3, 0, 3), work set-up row of wickerwork patt over center 80 (88, 96, 104, 120, 128) sts, k1 (0, 1, 3, 0, 3).

Keeping sts at each side of patt in rev St st (purl RS rows; knit WS rows) until you can work them into the pattern (see

Notes), cont in established patt until wickerwork section measures 2½" (6.5 cm) and piece measures 15¾" (40 cm) from hem fold line, ending with a WS row.

INC ROW: (RS) Keeping in patt, work 1 st, M1 (see Glossary), work in patt to last st, M1, work 1 st—2 sts inc'd.

Working new sts into wickerwork patt as they become available, [work 9 rows even, then rep inc row] 2 times—88 (94, 104, 116, 126, 140) sts. Work even until piece measures 20½" (52 cm) from hem fold line, ending with a WS row.

Shape Armholes

BO 5 (5, 6, 8, 10, 10) sts at beg of next 2 rows—78 (84, 92, 100, 106, 120) sts rem.

DEC ROW: (RS) Keeping in patt, work 1 st, ssk, work in patt to last 3 sts, k2tog, work 1 st—2 sts dec'd.

[Work 1 WS row even, then rep the dec row] 4 (5, 6, 8, 9, 14) times—68 (72, 78, 82, 86, 90) sts rem. Work even until armholes measures 5¾ (6, 6¼, 6¾, 7¼, 7¾)" (14.5 [15, 16, 17, 18.5, 19.5] cm), ending with a WS row.

NEXT ROW: (RS) Work 13 (13, 16, 17, 19, 21) sts in wickerwork patt, pm, p0 (0, 0, 1, 1, 1), [k2, p2] 10 (11, 11, 11, 11, 11) times, k2, p0 (0, 0, 0, 1, 1), pm, work 13 (13, 16, 17, 19, 21) sts in wickerwork patt—42 (46, 46, 48, 48, 48) center sts in rib patt between m.

Work 1 WS row even, working sts at each side in established wickerwork patt and rib sts between m as they appear—armholes measure 6 (6¼, 6½, 7, 7½, 8)" (15 [16, 16.5, 18, 19, 20.5] cm).

Shape Back Neck and Shoulders

With RS facing, work 15 (15, 18, 19, 21, 23) sts in patt, BO center 38 (42, 42, 44, 44, 44) sts, work in patt to end—15 (15, 18, 19, 21, 23) sts rem each side; place sts of right back neck on holder or allow them to rest on needle while working the left back neck.

Left Back Neck and Shoulder

Working on sts of left back neck only, work 1 WS row even.

DEC ROW: (RS) Ssk, work to end—1 st dec'd.

Work 1 WS row even in patt, then rep the dec row—13 (13, 16, 17, 19, 21) sts rem; no rib sts rem at neck edge. Work even until armhole measures 6¾ (7, 7¼, 7¾, 8¼, 8¾)" (17 [18, 18.5, 19.5, 21, 22] cm), ending with a WS row. Shape shoulder using short-rows (see Glossary) as foll:

SHORT-ROW 1: (RS) Work to last 5 (5, 6, 6, 7, 7) sts, wrap next st, turn work.

SHORT-ROW 2: (WS) Work in patt to end.

SHORT-ROW 3: Work to last 9 (9, 11, 12, 13, 14) sts, wrap next st, turn.

SHORT-ROW 4: Work in patt to end.

NEXT ROW: (RS) Work across all sts, working wraps tog with wrapped sts.

Place sts on holder.

Right Back Neck and Shoulder

Return 15 (15, 18, 19, 21, 23) held right back neck sts to needle if they are not already on the needle, and rejoin yarn with WS facing at neck edge. Work 1 WS row even in patt.

DEC ROW: (RS) Work to last 2 sts, k2tog—1 st dec'd.

Work 1 WS row even in patt, then rep the dec row—13 (13, 17, 19, 21) sts rem; no rib sts rem at neck edge. Work even until armhole measures 6¾ (7, 7¼, 7¾, 8¼, 8¾)" (17 [18, 18.5, 19.5, 21, 22] cm), ending with a RS row. Shape shoulder using short-rows as foll:

SHORT-ROW 1: (WS) Work to last 5 (5, 6, 6, 7, 7) sts, wrap next st, turn.

SHORT-ROW 2: (RS) Work in patt to end.

SHORT-ROW 3: Work to last 9 (9, 11, 12, 13, 14) sts, wrap next st, turn.

SHORT-ROW 4: Work in patt to end.

NEXT ROW: (WS) Work across all sts, working wraps tog with wrapped sts.

Place sts on holder.

Front

Work as for back until armholes measure 4 (4¼, 4½, 5, 5½, 6)" (10 [11, 11.5, 12.5, 14, 15] cm), ending with a WS row—68 (72, 78, 82, 86, 90) sts.

Shape Front Neck and Shoulders

DIVIDING ROW: (RS) Keeping in patt, work 27 (27, 30, 31, 33, 35) sts, pm, [k2, p2] 1 (2, 2, 2, 2, 2) time(s), k2 (1, 1, 2, 2, 2), p1 (0, 0, 0, 0, 0)—34 (36, 39, 41, 43, 45) left front neck sts worked; place rem 34 (36, 39, 41, 43, 45) sts on holder for right front neck or allow them to rest on needle while working the left front neck.

Left Front Neck and Shoulder

Work left front sts as foll:

ROW 1: (WS) Work 7 (9, 9, 10, 10, 10) rib sts as they appear to m, sl m, work in wickerwork patt to end.

ROW 2: (RS) Work in wickerwork patt to 6 sts before m, place new m, p2, k2, p2, remove previous m, work in rib patt to end—13 (15, 15, 16, 16, 16) sts in rib patt at neck edge.

ROWS 3, 5, 7, AND 9: Work rib sts as they appear to m, sl m, work in wickerwork patt to end.

ROW 4: Work in wickerwork patt to 4 sts before m, place new m, p2, k2, remove previous m, work in rib patt to end—17 (19, 19, 20, 20, 20) sts in rib patt at neck edge.

ROW 6: Work in wickerwork patt to 2 sts before m, place new m, k2, remove previous m, work in rib patt to end—19 (21, 21, 22, 22, 22) sts in rib patt at neck edge.

ROW 8: Work in wickerwork patt to 2 sts before m, place new m, p2, remove previous m, work in rib patt to end—21 (23, 23, 24, 24, 24) sts in rib patt at neck edge; 13 (13, 16, 17, 19, 21) wickerwork sts.

ROWS 10–12: Work even in patt, beg and ending with a RS row—front neck slit measures 1½" (3.8 cm) from dividing row.

Keeping in patt, BO 7 (9, 9, 10, 10, 10) sts at beg of next WS row, then BO 6 sts at beg of foll WS row, then BO 4 sts at beg of next WS row, then BO 2 sts at beg of next 2 WS rows—13 (13, 16, 17, 19, 21) sts rem; no rib sts rem at neck edge. Work even in patt until armhole measures 6¾ (7, 7¼, 7¾, 8¼, 8¾)" (17 [18, 18.5, 19.5, 21, 22] cm), ending with a RS row. Shape shoulder using short-rows as for right back shoulder.

Place sts on holder.

Right Front Neck and Shoulder

Return 34 (36, 39, 41, 43, 45) held right front neck sts to needle if they are not already on the needle and rejoin yarn with RS facing at neck edge.

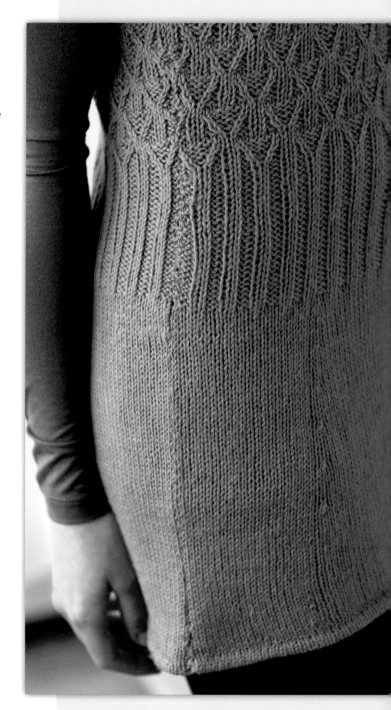

ROW 1: (RS) P1 (0, 0, 0, 0, 0), k2 (1, 1, 2, 2, 2), [p2, k2] 1 (2, 2, 2, 2, 2) time(s), pm, work 27 (27, 30, 31, 33, 35) sts in wickerwork patt—7 (9, 9, 10, 10, 10) rib sts at neck edge.

ROWS 2, 4, 6, AND 8: (WS) Work in wickerwork patt to m, sl m, work in rib patt to end.

ROW 3: Work in rib patt to m, remove m, p2, k2, p2, place new m, work in wickerwork patt to end—13 (15, 15, 16, 16, 16) sts in rib patt at neck edge.

ROW 5: Work in rib patt to m, remove m, k2, p2, place new m, work in wickerwork patt to end—17 (19, 19, 20, 20, 20) sts in rib patt at neck edge.

ROW 7: Work in rib patt to m, remove m, k2, place new m, work in wickerwork patt to end—19 (21, 21, 22, 22, 22) sts in rib patt at neck edge.

ROW 9: Work in rib patt to m, remove m, p2, place new m, work in wickerwork patt to end—21 (23, 23, 24, 24, 24) sts in rib patt at neck edge; 13 (13, 16, 17, 19, 21) wickerwork sts.

ROWS 10–12: Work even in patt, beg and ending with a WS row—front neck slit measures 1½″ (3.8 cm) from dividing row.

Keeping in patt, BO 7 (9, 9, 10, 10, 10) sts at beg of next RS row, then BO 6 sts at beg of foll RS row, then BO 4 sts at beg of next RS row, then BO 2 sts at beg of next 2 RS rows—13 (13, 16, 17, 19, 21) sts rem; no rib sts rem at neck edge. Work even in patt until armhole measures 6¾ (7, 7¼, 7¾, 8¼, 8¾)″ (17 [18, 18.5, 19.5, 21, 22] cm), ending with a WS row. Shape shoulder using short-rows as for left back shoulder.

Place sts on holder.

Finishing

Block pieces to measurements. With RS touching and WS facing outward, use the three-needle method (see Glossary) to BO the 13 (13, 16, 17, 19, 21) front and back shoulder sts tog at each side. With yarn threaded on a tapestry needle, sew side seams, matching patts.

Weave in loose ends. Block again if desired.

AnnaMaria
CARDIGAN

This refined cardigan, worked in a luxurious blend of merino and cashmere, is ideal for seasonal transitions when it's too warm for fleece but too cold for an openwork wrap. The body is knitted in one piece from the bottom up, with the front bands worked along the way. The set-in sleeves are picked up and worked down from the armholes, leaving just minimal finishing after the last stitch is bound off. The carved diamond pattern along each front edge continues around the back neck and adds a bit of textural interest to the classic look.

FINISHED SIZE

$30^3/_4$ ($33^3/_4$, 38, 41, $45^1/_4$, $48^1/_4$, $52^3/_4$)" (78 [85.5, 96.5, 104, 115, 122.5, 134] cm) bust circumference, buttoned with $^1/_2$" (1.3 cm) front bands overlapped.

Sweater shown measures $33^3/_4$" (85.5 cm).

yarn
DK weight (#3 Light).

SHOWN HERE: Karabella Margrite (80% extrafine merino wool, 20% cashmere; 154 yd [141 m]/50 g): #13 red, 6 (6, 7, 8, 8, 9, 10) skeins.

needles
Body and sleeves: U.S. size 6 (4 mm): 24" (60 cm) circular (cir) and set of 4 or 5 double-pointed (dpn).

Edgings: U.S. size 5 (3.75 mm): 24" (60 cm) cir and set of 4 or 5 dpn.

Adjust needle sizes if necessary to obtain the correct gauge.

notions
Markers (m); cable needle (cn); stitch holders; tapestry needle; seven $^1/_2$" (1.3 cm) buttons.

gauge
22 sts and 34 rows = 4" (10 cm) in St st on larger needles.

10 sts of Right and Left Front Triangle charts measure $1^1/_4$" (3.2 cm) wide on larger needles.

4 garter sts at each front edge measure $^1/_2$" (1.3 cm) wide on larger needles.

NOTES

» The body is worked in one piece to the armholes, then the fronts and back are worked separately to the shoulders. The garter-stitch button- and buttonhole bands are worked at the same time as the body. Stitches for the sleeves are picked up around the armholes; the caps are shaped with short-rows, then the sleeves are worked in the round to the cuffs.

» The body circumferences shown on the schematic are with the fronts overlapped ½" (1.3 cm).

Body

With smaller cir needle, CO 181 (197, 221, 237, 261, 277, 301) sts. Do not join. Knit 6 rows, ending with a WS row. Change to larger cir needle.

ROW 1: (RS) K4 for garter st front band, work Row 1 of Right Front Triangle chart (page 78) over 10 sts, k32 (36, 42, 46, 52, 56, 62) right front sts, place marker (pm), sl 1 purlwise with yarn in back (pwise wyb) for right "seam" st, pm, k87 (95, 107, 115, 127, 135, 147) back sts, pm, sl 1 pwise wyb for left "seam" st, pm, k32 (36, 42, 46, 52, 56, 62) left front sts, work Row 1 of Left Front Triangle chart (page 78) over 10 sts, k4 for garter st front band.

ROW 2: (WS) K4, work Row 2 of chart over 10 sts, [purl to marked seam st, slip marker (sl m), p1, sl m] 2 times, purl to last 14 sts, work Row 2 of chart over 10 sts, k4.

ROW 3: (RS; buttonhole row) K2, k2tog, yo, work Row 3 of chart over 10 sts, [knit to marked seam st, sl m, sl 1 pwise wyb, sl m] 2 times, knit to last 14 sts, work Row 3 of chart over 10 sts, k4.

NOTE: Work 6 more buttonholes by working [k2, k2tog, yo] at beg of every 18th row 6 more times; i.e., on Rows 21 (39, 57, 75, 93, 111). Keep track of the buttonhole spacing separate from the 20-row chart patts to make sure that you do not accidentally work past a buttonhole position.

NEXT ROW: (WS) K4, cont chart patt over 10 sts, [purl to seam st, sl m, p1, sl m] 2 times purl to last 14 sts, cont chart patt over 10 sts, k4.

NEXT ROW: (RS) K4, cont chart patt over 10 sts, [knit to seam st, sl m, sl 1 pwise wyb, sl m] 2 times, knit to last 14 sts, cont chart patt over 10 sts, k4.

Working any required buttonholes, rep the last 2 rows until piece measure 3" (7.5 cm) from CO, ending with a RS row.

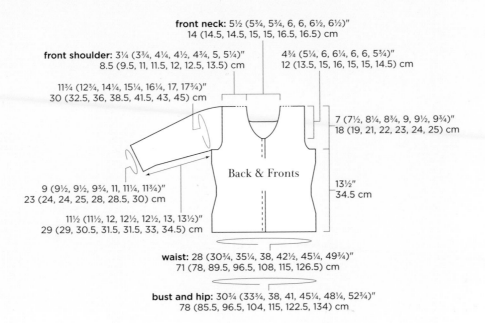

front neck: 5½ (5¾, 5¾, 6, 6, 6½, 6½)"
14 (14.5, 14.5, 15, 15, 16.5, 16.5) cm

front shoulder: 3¼ (3¾, 4¼, 4½, 4¾, 5, 5¼)"
8.5 (9.5, 11, 11.5, 12, 12.5, 13.5) cm

4¾ (5¼, 6, 6¼, 6, 6, 5¾)"
12 (13.5, 15, 16, 15, 15, 14.5) cm

11¾ (12¾, 14¼, 15¼, 16¼, 17, 17¾)"
30 (32.5, 36, 38.5, 41.5, 43, 45) cm

7 (7½, 8¼, 8¾, 9, 9½, 9¾)"
18 (19, 21, 22, 23, 24, 25) cm

Back & Fronts

13½"
34.5 cm

9 (9½, 9½, 9¾, 11, 11¼, 11¾)"
23 (24, 24, 25, 28, 28.5, 30) cm

11½ (11½, 12, 12½, 12½, 13, 13½)"
29 (29, 30.5, 31.5, 31.5, 33, 34.5) cm

waist: 28 (30¾, 35¼, 38, 42½, 45¼, 49¾)"
71 (78, 89.5, 96.5, 108, 115, 126.5) cm

bust and hip: 30¾ (33¾, 38, 41, 45¼, 48¼, 52¾)"
78 (85.5, 96.5, 104, 115, 122.5, 134) cm

Shape Waist

Place dart markers (m) on next row as foll:

NEXT ROW: (WS) K4, work 10 sts chart patt, p15 (17, 21, 23, 27, 29, 33), pm for left front dart, p17 (19, 21, 23, 25, 27, 29), sl m, p1, sl m, p17 (19, 21, 23, 25, 27, 29), pm for left back dart, p53 (57, 65, 69, 77, 81, 89), pm for right back dart, p17 (19, 21, 23, 25, 27, 29), sl m, p1, sl m, p17 (19, 21, 23, 25, 27, 29), pm for right front dart, p15 (17, 21, 23, 27, 29, 33), work 10 sts chart patt, k4.

DEC ROW: (RS) Work to 2 sts before right front dart m, k2tog, sl m, work to right back dart m m, sl m, ssk, work to 2 sts before left back dart m, k2tog, sl m, work to left front dart m, sl m, ssk, work to end—4 sts dec'd.

Working buttonholes as required, [work 7 rows even, then rep the dec row] 3 times—165 (181, 205, 221, 245, 261, 285) sts rem. Work even until piece measures 7½" (19 cm) from CO, ending with a WS row.

INC ROW: (RS) Work to right front dart m, M1 (see Glossary), sl m, work to right back dart m, sl m, M1, work to left back dart m, M1, sl m, work to left front dart m, sl m, M1, work to end—4 sts inc'd.

Working buttonholes as required, [work 9 rows even, then rep the inc row] 3 times—181 (197, 221, 237, 261, 277, 301) sts. Work even until 7th buttonhole row has been completed, then work 1 WS row even, removing seam and dart markers in last row—piece measures 13½" (34.5 cm) from CO.

Divide for Fronts and Back

With RS facing and keeping in patts, work 47 (51, 57, 61, 67, 71, 77) right front sts, BO 4 (5, 6, 7, 9, 9, 10) sts for right underarm, work until there are 83 (90, 101, 108, 118, 126, 137) back sts on needle after BO gap, turn work—47 (51, 57, 61, 67, 71, 77) right front sts before BO gap, 83 (90, 101, 108, 118, 126, 137) back sts; 47 (51, 57, 61, 67, 71, 77) left front sts rem unworked at end of needle. Place sts for each front on separate holder or allow them to rest on needle while working the back sts.

Back

Cont on 83 (90, 101, 108, 118, 126, 137) back sts as foll:

NEXT ROW: (WS) BO 4 (5, 6, 7, 9, 9, 10) sts, work to end—79 (85, 95, 101, 109, 117, 127) sts rem.

DEC ROW: (RS) K1, ssk, work to last 3 sts, k2tog, k1—2 sts dec'd.

[Work 1 WS row even, then rep the dec row] 4 (4, 6, 7, 9, 11, 14) times—69 (75, 81, 85, 89, 93, 97) sts rem. Work even until armhole measures 4½ (5, 5¾, 6¼, 6½, 7, 7¼)" (11.5 [12.5, 14.5, 16, 16.5, 18, 18.5] cm), ending with a WS row.

Shape Neck

With RS facing, k26 (28, 31, 32, 34, 35, 37), BO center 17 (19, 19, 21, 21, 23, 23) sts, knit to end—26 (28, 31, 32, 34, 35, 37) sts each side.

Place sts for right neck on holder or allow them to rest on needle while working the left neck sts.

Left Side

Working 26 (28, 31, 32, 34, 35, 37) left neck sts only, purl 1 WS row. At neck edge (beg of RS rows), BO 6 sts once, then BO 4 sts once, then BO 3 sts once—13 (15, 18, 19, 21, 22, 24) sts rem. Work 1 WS row even.

DEC ROW: (RS) K1, ssk, knit to end—1 st dec'd.

[Work 1 WS row even, then rep the dec row] 3 times—9 (11, 14, 15, 17, 18, 20) sts rem. Work even until armhole measures 7 (7½, 8¼, 8¾, 9, 9½, 9¾)" (18 [19, 21, 22, 23, 24, 25] cm), ending with a WS row. Place sts on holder.

NOTE: The neck and shoulder widths shown on the schematic represent the front shoulder width (including the triangle pattern and front band) and the distance between the front edges at the shoulder line. For blocking purposes, the held back shoulder sts measure about 1¾ (2, 2½, 2¾, 3, 3¼, 3¾)" (4.5 [5, 6.5, 7, 7.5, 8.5, 9.5] cm) wide.

knit on RS; purl on WS

sl 1 st onto cn and hold in back, k1, k1 from cn

sl 1 st onto cn and hold in front, k1, k1 from cn

Left Front Triangle

Right Front Triangle

Right Side

Return 26 (28, 31, 32, 34, 35, 37) held right neck sts to needle, if they are not already on the needle, and rejoin yarn with WS facing at neck edge. At neck edge (beg of WS rows), BO 6 sts once, then BO 4 sts once, then BO 3 sts once—13 (15, 18, 19, 21, 22, 24) sts rem.

DEC ROW: (RS) Knit to last 3 sts, k2tog, k1—1 st dec'd.

[Work 1 WS row even, then rep the dec row] 3 times—9 (11, 14, 15, 17, 18, 20) sts rem.

Work even until armhole measures 7 (7½, 8¼, 8¾, 9, 9½, 9¾)" (18 [19, 21, 22, 23, 24, 25] cm), ending with a WS row.

Place sts on holder.

[Work 1 WS row even, then rep the dec row] 4 (4, 6, 7, 9, 11, 14) times—38 (41, 44, 46, 48, 50, 52) sts rem. Work even in patt until armhole measures 2¼ (2¼, 2¼, 2½, 3, 3½, 4)" (5.5 [5.5, 5.5, 6.5, 7.5, 9, 10] cm), ending with a WS row.

Shape Neck

NEXT ROW: (RS) K4 front edge sts, work 10 sts in chart patt, k1, ssk, knit to end—1 st dec'd.

NEXT ROW: (WS) Purl to last 17 sts, p2tog through the back loops (tbl), p1, work 10 chart sts, k4 front edge sts—1 st dec'd.

Rep the last 2 rows 2 more times, then work RS dec row once more—31 (34, 37, 39, 41, 43, 45) sts rem.

NEXT ROW: (WS) Purl to last 14 sts, work 10 chart sts, k4.

DEC ROW: (RS) K4, work 10 chart sts, k1, ssk, knit to end—1 st dec'd.

[Work 1 WS row even, the rep the dec row] 3 (4, 4, 5, 5, 6, 6) times—27 (29, 32, 33, 35, 36, 38) sts rem. Work dec row every 4th row (i.e., every other RS row) 4 times—23 (25, 28, 29, 31, 32, 34) sts rem. Work even until armhole measures 7 (7½, 8¼, 8¾, 9, 9½, 9¾)" (18 [19, 21, 22, 23, 24, 25] cm), ending with a WS row. Place 9 (11, 14, 15, 17, 18, 20) shoulder sts on one holder and place rem 14 sts of front edge and chart patt on a separate holder. Make a note of the last chart row completed so you can resume the patt with the correct row later for back neckband.

Left Front

Return 47 (51, 57, 61, 67, 71, 77) held left front sts to needle, if they are not already on the needle, and rejoin yarn with RS facing at armhole edge.

NEXT ROW: (RS) BO 4 (5, 6, 7, 9, 9, 10) sts, work in patt to end—43 (46, 51, 54, 58, 62, 67) sts rem.

Work 1 WS row even.

DEC ROW: (RS) K1, ssk, work in patt to end—1 st dec'd.

[Work 1 WS row even, then rep the dec row] 4 (4, 6, 7, 9, 11, 14) times—38 (41, 44, 46, 48, 50, 52) sts rem. Work even in patt until armhole measures 2¼ (2¼, 2¼, 2½, 3, 3½, 4)" (5.5 [5.5, 5.5, 6.5, 7.5, 9, 10] cm), ending with a WS row.

NOTE: For blocking purposes, the entire back neck between the two groups of held shoulder sts measures about 9¼ (9¾, 9¾, 10, 10, 10¼, 10¼)" (23.5 [25, 25, 25.5, 25.5, 26, 26] cm) wide before applying the neckband.

Right Front

Return 47 (51, 57, 61, 67, 71, 77) held right front sts to needle, if they are not already on the needle, and rejoin yarn with WS facing at armhole edge.

NEXT ROW: (WS) BO 4 (5, 6, 7, 9, 9, 10) sts, work in patt to end—43 (46, 51, 54, 58, 62, 67) sts rem.

DEC ROW: (RS) Work in patt to last 3 sts, k2tog, k1—1 st dec'd.

Shape Neck

NEXT ROW: (RS) Knit to last 17 sts, k2tog, k1, work last 14 sts in patt—1 st dec'd.

NEXT ROW: (WS) Work first 14 sts in patt, p1, p2tog, purl to end—1 st dec'd.

Rep the last 2 rows 2 more times, then work RS dec row once more—31 (34, 37, 39, 41, 43, 45) sts rem.

NEXT ROW: (WS) Work 14 sts in patt, purl to end.

DEC ROW: (RS) Knit to last 17 sts, k2tog, k1, work 14 sts in patt—1 st dec'd.

[Work 1 WS row even, the rep the dec row] 3 (4, 4, 5, 5, 6, 6) times—27 (29, 32, 33, 35, 36, 38) sts rem. Work dec row every 4th row (i.e., every other RS row) 4 times—23 (25, 28, 29, 31, 32, 34) sts rem. Work even until armhole measures 7 (7½, 8¼, 8¾, 9, 9½, 9¾)" (18 [19, 21, 22, 23, 24, 25] cm), ending with the same WS chart row as right front. Place 9 (11, 14, 15, 17, 18, 20) shoulder sts on one holder and place rem 14 sts of front edge and chart patt on a separate holder.

Join Shoulders

Block body to measurements. With RS touching and WS facing outward, use the three-needle method (see Glossary) to BO 9 (11, 14, 15, 17, 18, 20) front and back shoulder sts tog at each side—14 sts of front band and chart patt rem on holders at each side.

Sleeves

With larger cir needle, RS facing, and beg at shoulder seam, pick up and knit 28 (30, 33, 35, 36, 38, 39) sts evenly spaced along armhole opening to beg of underarm BO, pm, pick up and knit 8 (10, 12, 14, 18, 18, 20) sts along armhole BO, pm, pick up and knit 28 (30, 33, 35, 36, 38, 39) sts evenly spaced to shoulder seam, pm—64 (70, 78, 84, 90, 94, 98) sts total. Work short-rows (see Glossary) to shape cap as foll:

SHORT-ROW 1: (RS) K5, wrap next st, turn.

SHORT-ROW 2: (WS) P5 to shoulder join m, sl m, p5, wrap next st, turn.

SHORT-ROW 3: K5, sl m, k9 working wrap tog with wrapped st, wrap next st, turn.

SHORT-ROW 4: P9, sl m, p9 working wrap tog with wrapped st, wrap next st, turn.

SHORT-ROW 5: K9, sl m, k12 working wrap tog with wrapped st, wrap next st, turn.

SHORT-ROW 6: P12, sl m, p12 working wrap tog with wrapped st, wrap next st, turn.

SHORT-ROW 7: K12, sl m, k13 working wrap tog with wrapped st, wrap next st, turn.

SHORT-ROW 8: P13, sl m, p13 working wrap tog with wrapped st, wrap next st, turn—last wrapped st at each side is the 14th st from shoulder join m.

SHORT-ROW 9: Sl m as you come to it, knit to previously wrapped st, work wrap tog with wrapped st, wrap next st, turn—wrapped st is 1 st farther from shoulder join m.

SHORT-ROW 10: Sl m as you come to it, purl to previously wrapped st, work wrap tog with wrapped st, wrap next st, turn—wrapped st is 1 st farther from shoulder join m.

Rep the last 2 rows 13 (15, 18, 20, 21, 23, 24) more times—last wrapped st at each side is the st next to m on each side of underarm sts.

NEXT ROW: (RS) Knit to shoulder m, remove m, knit to wrapped st, work wrap tog with wrapped st, remove m, k4 (5, 6, 7, 9, 9, 10) to center of underarm, pm for center of underarm.

NEXT RND: Change to larger dpn. With RS still facing, knit 1 rnd on all sts, working wrap tog with wrapped st and ending at underarm m—sleeve cap measures 4½ (5, 5¾, 6, 6¼, 6¾, 7)" (11.5 [12.5, 14.5, 15, 16, 17, 18] cm) from pick-up row, measured straight up along a single column of sts in center of cap.

Knit 4 rnds even.

DEC RND: K1, ssk, knit to last 3 sts, k2tog, k1—2 sts dec'd.

Cont in St st, rep the dec rnd every 0 (10, 7, 6, 6, 6, 6) rnds 0 (2, 7, 11, 11, 12, 12) times, then every 9 (9, 6, 5, 5, 5, 5) rnds 6 (6, 5, 3, 3, 3, 4) times—50 (52, 52, 54, 60, 62, 64) sts rem. Work even until sleeve measures 10¾ (10¾, 11¼, 11¾, 11¾, 12¼, 12¾)" (27.5 [27.5, 28.5, 30, 30, 31, 32.5] cm) from joining rnd. Change to smaller dpn. [Knit 1 rnd, purl 1 rnd] 3 times—sleeve measures 11½ (11½, 12, 12½, 12½, 13, 13½)" (29 [29, 30.5, 31.5, 31.5, 33, 34.5] cm) from joining rnd. BO all sts.

Finishing

Back Neckband

Place 14 held right front band sts on smaller needle and join yarn with RS facing at front edge.

SET-UP ROW: (RS) Work 14 sts in established patt, M1 (selvedge st for seaming)—15 sts.

Working new selvedge st in St st, cont in patt and work 2 rows even, ending with a RS row. Maintaining patt as well as possible, work short-rows as foll:

SHORT-ROW 1: (WS) Work 10 sts in patt, wrap next st, turn work.

SHORT-ROW 2: (RS) Work in patt to end.

SHORT-ROW 3: Work in patt to end, working wrap tog with wrapped st when you come to it.

SHORT-ROW 4: Work in patt to end.

Rep Short-rows 1–4 six more times. Work even in patt until band reaches to center back neck when slightly stretched, ending with a RS row (ideally, Row 9 or 19 of chart).

Place sts on holder.

Place 14 held left front band sts on smaller needle and join yarn with RS facing at neck edge.

SET-UP ROW: (RS) M1 (selvedge st for seaming), work 14 sts in established patt, M1—15 sts.

Working new selvedge st in St st, cont in patt and work 1 WS row even. Maintaining patt as well as possible, work short-rows as foll:

SHORT-ROW 1: (RS) Work 10 sts in patt, wrap next st, turn work.

SHORT-ROW 2: (WS) Work in patt to end.

SHORT-ROW 3: Work in patt to end, working wrap tog with wrapped st when you come to it.

SHORT-ROW 4: Work in patt to end.

Rep Short-rows 1–4 six more times. Work even in patt until band reaches to center back neck when slightly stretched, ending with the same RS chart row as right neckband.

With RS touching and WS facing outward, use the three-needle method to BO sts tog. With yarn threaded on a tapestry needle, sew selvedge of neckband to back neck edge.

Weave in loose ends. Block again, if desired. Sew buttons to left front band, opposite buttonholes.

Jennifer
SHELL

Knitted from side to side, this simple vest makes the most of the drapey fabric created by a blend of alpaca and cotton. With a center neck notch and playful graduated pleats worked after the body is completed, this vest is my interpretation of a woman's tuxedo shirt. The pleats are strategically placed around the neckline to draw the eye upward toward the wearer's face. Work it in a smaller size to wear alone as a shell or in a larger size to layer as a vest. Either way, this casual piece is light and comfortable.

FINISHED SIZE
About 33 (35, 38, 43, 47, 50)" (84 [89, 96.5, 109, 119.5, 127] cm) bust circumference.

Shell shown measures 35" (89 cm).

yarn
Sportweight (#2 Fine).

SHOWN HERE: Manos Serena (60% alpaca, 40% cotton; 170 yd [155 m]/50 g): #2246 oyster (taupe), 4 (4, 4, 5, 5, 6) skeins.

needles
BODY: size U.S. 5 (3.75 mm): 24" (60 cm) circular (cir).

PLEATS: size U.S. 4 (3.5 mm): 24" (60 cm) cir.

Adjust needle size if necessary to obtain the correct gauge.

notions
Waste yarn for provisional CO; markers (m); stitch holders; size F/5 (3.75 mm) crochet hook; spare needle in same size as smaller cir needle for finishing pleats; tapestry needle.

gauge
23 sts and 33 rows = 4" (10 cm) in St st on larger needles.

NOTES

» The pleat locations are marked by lines of purl stitches worked on the front. During finishing, stitches are picked up along these placement lines and worked in stockinette for several rows, then each pleat is folded in half and secured by working its live stitches together with stitches from the base of the pleat.

Back

With waste yarn and larger needle, use a provisional method (see Glossary) to CO 89 sts. Work even in St st (knit RS rows; purl WS rows) until piece measures 1 (1¼, 1¼, 1½, 1¾, 2)" (2.5 [3.2, 3.2, 3.8, 4.5, 5] cm), ending with a WS row (about 8 [10, 10, 12, 14, 16] rows).

Shape Right Back Armhole

INC ROW: (RS) K1, M1 (see Glossary), knit to end—1 st inc'd.

[Work 1 WS row even, then rep inc row] 3 (3, 5, 7, 9, 9) times—93 (93, 95, 97, 99, 99) sts. Work 1 WS row even.

NEXT ROW: (RS) Use the knitted method (see Glossary) to CO 35 (38, 39, 41, 42, 43) sts at beg of row, knit across newly CO sts, then knit to end—128 (131, 134, 138, 141, 142) sts total; piece measures about 2 (2¼, 2¾, 3½, 4¼, 4½)" (5 [5.5, 7, 9, 11, 11.5] cm) from CO.

Right Shoulder

Cont even in St st until right back shoulder measures 3¼ (3½, 3¾, 4¼, 4½, 5)" (8.5 [9, 9.5, 11, 11.5, 12.5] cm) from sts CO for armhole shaping and about 5¼ (5¾, 6½, 7¾, 8¾, 9½)" (13.5 [14.5, 16.5, 19.5, 22, 24] cm) from initial CO, ending with a WS row.

Shape Back Neck

DEC ROW: (RS) K1, ssk, knit to end—1 st dec'd.

[Work 1 WS row even, then rep dec row] 2 times—125 (128, 131, 135, 138, 139) sts rem. Work even until neck measures 5½" (14 cm) from first dec row at start of neck shaping (about 45 rows), ending with a WS row.

INC ROW: (RS) K1, M1, knit to end—1 st inc'd.

[Work 1 WS row even, then rep the inc row] 2 times—128 (131, 134, 138, 141, 142) sts; piece measures 6" (15 cm) from first dec row at start of neck shaping (about 50 rows total for back neck).

Left Shoulder

Work even until left back shoulder measures 3¼ (3½, 3¾, 4¼, 4½, 5)" (8.5 [9, 9.5, 11, 11.5, 12.5] cm) final inc row at end of back neck shaping, ending with a WS row.

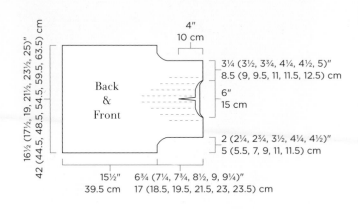

Shape Left Back Armhole

NEXT ROW: (RS) BO 35 (38, 39, 41, 42, 43) sts, knit to end—93 (93, 95, 97, 99, 99) sts rem.

Work 1 WS row even.

DEC ROW: (RS) K1, ssk, knit to end—1 st dec'd.

[Work 1 WS row even, then rep the dec row] 3 (3, 5, 7, 9, 9) times—89 sts rem for all sizes. Work even until piece measures 1 (1¼, 1¼, 1½, 1¾, 2)" (2.5 [3.2, 3.2, 3.8, 4.5, 5] cm) from last dec row, ending with a WS row (about 8 [10, 10, 12, 14, 16] rows)—piece measures 2 (2¼, 2¾, 3½, 4¼, 4½)" (5 [5.5, 7, 9, 11, 11.5] cm) from sts BO for left back armhole and 16½ (17½, 19, 21½, 23½, 25)" (42 [44.5, 48.5, 54.5, 59.5, 63.5] cm) total from initial CO. Cut yarn and place live sts on holder for joining to front later.

Front

With waste yarn and larger needle, use a provisional method to CO 89 sts.

Shape Left Front Armhole

Work as for back to end of right back armhole shaping, then work 1 WS row after armhole CO row—128 (131, 134, 138, 141, 142) sts; piece measures about 2 (2¼, 2¾, 3½, 4¼, 4½)" (5 [5.5, 7, 9, 11, 11.5] cm) from CO.

Pleat Placement and Neck Shaping

NEXT ROW: (RS) K39 (42, 45, 49, 52, 53), pm for pleats, knit to end.

Cont even in St st until left front shoulder measures 2¾ (3, 3¼, 3¾, 4, 4½)" (7 [7.5, 8.5, 9.5, 10, 11.5] cm) from sts CO at end of armhole shaping, ending with a WS row. Work neck shaping and lines of purl sts for pleat placement as foll (see Notes):

ROW 1: (RS; pleat row) K2, purl to 11 sts before m, k11, slip marker (sl m), knit to end.

ROWS 2-4: Work even in St st—shoulder measures 3¼ (3½, 3¾, 4¼, 4½, 5)" 8.5 [9, 9.5, 11, 11.5, 12.5] cm) from sts CO at end of armhole shaping.

ROWS 5 AND 7: (neck dec rows) K1, ssk, knit to end—1 st dec'd at neck edge in each row.

ROWS 6 AND 8: Purl.

ROW 9: (pleat and neck dec row) K1, ssk, purl to m, sl m, knit to end—1 st dec'd.

ROWS 10 AND 12: Purl.

ROWS 11 AND 13: (neck dec rows) K1, ssk, knit to end—1 st dec'd in each row; 123 (126, 129, 133, 136, 137) sts rem after Row 13.

ROWS 14-16: Work even in St st.

ROW 17: (pleat row) K2, purl to m, sl m, p11, knit to end.

ROWS 18–24: Work even in St st.

ROW 25: (pleat row) K2, purl to m, sl m, p22, knit to end.

ROWS 26–28: Work even in St st, removing pleat m as you come to it, and ending with a WS row—piece measures 3″ (7.5 cm) from first neck dec in Row 5 and shoulder measures 6¼ (6½, 6¾, 7¼, 7½, 8)″ (16 [16.5, 17, 18.5, 19, 20.5] cm) from sts CO at end of armhole shaping.

ROW 29: (RS) BO 17 sts, knit to end—106 (109, 112, 116, 119, 120) sts.

ROW 30: Purl to end, use the knitted method to CO 17 sts—123 (126, 129, 133, 136, 137) sts.

ROW 31: K34 (37, 40, 44, 47, 48), pm for pleats, knit to end.

ROW 32: Purl.

ROW 33: (pleat row) K2, purl to m, sl m, p22, knit to end.

ROWS 34–40: Work even in St st.

ROW 41: (pleat row) K2, purl to m, sl m, p11, knit to end.

ROWS 42–44: Work even in St st.

ROWS 45 AND 47: (neck inc rows) K1, M1, knit to end—1 st inc'd at neck edge in each row.

ROWS 46 AND 48: Purl.

ROW 49: (pleat and neck inc rows) K2, M1, purl to m, knit to end—1 st inc'd.

ROWS 50 AND 52: Purl.

ROWS 51 AND 53: (neck inc rows) K1, M1, knit to end—1 st inc'd in each row; 128 (131, 134, 138, 141, 142) sts after Row 53.

ROWS 54–56: Work even in St st.

ROW 57: (pleat row) K2, purl to 11 sts before m, k11, sl m, knit to end.

Work even until right front shoulder measures 3¼ (3½, 3¾, 4¼, 4½, 5)″ 8.5 [9, 9.5, 11, 11.5, 12.5] cm) from last neck inc in Row 53, ending with a WS row.

Shape Right Front Armhole

Work as for left back armhole—89 sts rem for all sizes. Work even until piece measures 1 (1¼, 1¼, 1½, 1¾, 2)″ (2.5 [3.2, 3.2, 3.8, 4.5, 5] cm) from last dec row, ending with a WS row (about 8 [10, 10, 12, 14, 16] rows)—piece measures 2 (2¼, 2¾, 3½, 4¼, 4½)″ (5 [5.5, 7, 9, 11, 11.5] cm) from sts BO for right front armhole and 16½ (17½, 19, 21½, 23½, 25)″ (42 [44.5, 48.5, 54.5, 59.5, 63.5] cm) total from initial CO. Cut yarn and place live sts on holder for joining to front later.

Finishing

Block pieces to measurements.

Pleats

NOTE: The finished pleats fold away from the center on each side of the front neck slit, so the left pleats fold toward the left armhole, and the right pleats fold toward the right armhole.

Left Front Pleats

Hold front sideways in the direction of knitting, with RS facing and shoulder edge on your right. Each purled placement line appears as a series of upper (frown) and lower (smile) bumps. With smaller needle, pick up and knit 1 st from each lower purl bump along one pleat placement line, picking up from the shoulder end of the line toward the lower body. Work in St st for 7 rows, beg and ending with a WS row. With RS facing, slip an empty needle from left to right through the upper purl bumps of the same placement line, making sure to pick up the same number of sts as on the pleat needle (these sts are just slipped on the needle, not picked up and knitted). Fold pleat in half with WS touching and RS facing outward and bring the two needles tog with the needle holding the live pleat sts in front.

NEXT ROW: (RS) P2tog (1 st from each needle), *p2tog, pass first st over the second st on right needle to BO; rep from * until all sts have been BO, then fasten off last st.

Work the rem 3 left front pleats in the same manner.

Right Front Pleats

Hold front sideways with RS facing so the shoulder edge is on your left. With smaller needle, pick up and knit 1 st from each lower purl bump along one pleat placement line, picking up from the lower body end of the line toward the shoulder. Work in St st for 7 rows, beg and ending with a WS row. Finish as for left front pleat. Work the rem 3 right front pleats in the same manner.

Fold pleats on each side away from the center and block again to flatten pleats as shown in photograph.

With yarn threaded on a tapestry needle, sew shoulder seams. Carefully remove waste yarn from provisional CO at sides and place 89 exposed sts on spare needle. With RS touching and WS facing outward, use the three-needle method (see Glossary) to BO the live front and back sts tog at the side "seams."

Edgings

With crochet hook and RS facing, work 1 rnd of single crochet (sc; see Glossary) around each armhole opening. Work 1 rnd of sc around lower edge. Work 1 rnd of sc around neck opening, working 3 sc in each corner at top of front neck slit.

Weave in loose ends.

Tulip HENLEY

Worked in a light, crisp cotton/linen blend ideally suited for hot-weather wear, this pretty cap-sleeved pullover features a Henley placket decorated with plump buds atop slender staggered stalks. The hem is punctuated with a delicate scalloped edging. To counteract the yarn's tendency to stretch, the front and back are worked in pieces that are seamed together, then the cap sleeves are worked from the top down and shaped with short-rows along the way. Button this Henley all the way to the neck for a demure crewneck look or leave some buttons unfastened for an open V.

FINISHED SIZE

About 31½ (34, 38½, 42½, 46½, 50½)" (80 [86.5, 98, 108, 118, 128.5] cm) bust circumference.

Sweater shown measures 34" (86.5 cm).

yarn

DK weight (#3 Light).

SHOWN HERE: Classic Elite Yarns Allegoro (70% cotton, 30% linen; 152 yd [139 m]/50 g): #5655 piccante (rust), 5 (6, 6, 7, 8, 8) skeins.

needles

U.S. size 4 (3.5 mm): 24" or 32" (60 or 80 cm) circular (cir) and set of 4 or 5 double-pointed (dpn).

Adjust needle size if necessary to obtain the correct gauge.

notions

Nine (nine, ten, ten, eleven, twelve) ⅜" (1 cm) buttons; markers (m); stitch holders; spare needle same size as main needle for three-needle bind-off; tapestry needle.

gauge

23 sts and 30 rows = 4" (10 cm) in St st.

stitch guide

Petite Shells Edging (multiple of 5 sts + 2, dec'd to multiple of 4 sts + 2)

ROW 1: (RS) K1, yo, *k5, sl 2nd, 3rd, 4th, and 5th sts on right needle over first st, yo; rep from * to last st, k1—st count has dec'd to a mult of 2 sts + 3.

ROW 2: (WS) P1, yo, *work [p1, yo, k1tbl] all in next st, p1; rep from *—st count has inc'd to a mult of 4 sts + 2.

ROW 3: K2, k1tbl, *k3, k1tbl; rep from * to last 3 sts, k3.

ROWS 4, 5, AND 6: Knit.

NOTES

» The stitch count of the Tulip chart does not remain constant from row to row. The pattern begins with a multiple of 8 stitches plus 1, increases gradually to a maximum of 18 stitches plus 11 in Row 15, then gradually decreases back to the starting stitch count in Row 20.

» The gray "no stitch" boxes in the Tulip chart act as placeholders where new stitches will be added or where these stitches will be decreased away again. When working the chart, skip over each "no stitch" symbol as you come to it; simply proceed to the next stitch.

» The shoulder widths do not increase all the way up the size range. This is because there are only two back neck widths with a jump of 2" (5 cm) between them. The three largest sizes all share the larger back neck, which makes the shoulder widths of the fourth and fifth sizes narrower than the shoulder width of the third size.

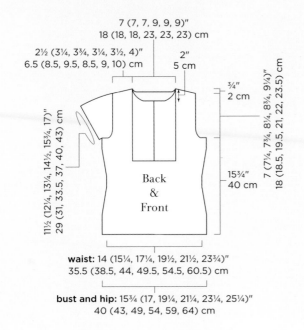

7 (7, 7, 9, 9, 9)"
18 (18, 18, 23, 23, 23) cm

2½ (3¼, 3¾, 3¼, 3½, 4)"
6.5 (8.5, 9.5, 8.5, 9, 10) cm

2"
5 cm

¾"
2 cm

7 (7¼, 7¾, 8¼, 8¾, 9¼)"
18 (18.5, 19.5, 21, 22, 23.5) cm

11½ (12¼, 13¼, 14½, 15¾, 17)"
29 (31, 33.5, 37, 40, 43) cm

Back & Front

15¾"
40 cm

waist: 14 (15¼, 17¼, 19½, 21½, 23¾)"
35.5 (38.5, 44, 49.5, 54.5, 60.5) cm

bust and hip: 15¾ (17, 19¼, 21¼, 23¼, 25¼)"
40 (43, 49, 54, 59, 64) cm

Back

With cir needle, CO 112 (122, 137, 152, 167, 182) sts. Work Rows 1–6 of petite shells edging (see Stitch Guide), ending with a WS row—90 (98, 110, 122, 134, 146) sts. Work even in St st (knit RS rows; purl WS rows) until piece measures 3¼" (8.5 cm) from CO, ending with a RS row.

SET-UP ROW: (WS) P18 (20, 22, 24, 27, 29), place marker (pm) for dart, p54 (58, 66, 74, 80, 88), pm for dart, p18 (20, 22, 24, 27, 29).

DEC ROW: (RS) Knit to m, slip marker (sl m), ssk, knit to 2 sts before next m, k2tog, sl m, knit to end—2 sts dec'd.

[Work 7 rows even, rep dec row] 4 times—80 (88, 100, 112, 124, 136) sts rem. Work even in St st until piece measures 9½" (24 cm) from CO, ending with a WS row.

INC ROW: (RS) Knit to m, sl m, M1 (see Glossary), knit to next m, M1, sl m, knit to end—2 sts inc'd.

[Work 7 rows even, rep inc row] 4 times—90 (98, 110, 122, 134, 146) sts. Work even until piece measures 15¾" (40 cm), ending with a WS row.

Shape Armholes

BO 4 (5, 6, 8, 9, 11) sts at beg of next 2 rows—82 (88, 98, 106, 116, 124) sts rem.

DEC ROW: (RS) K1, ssk, knit to last 3 sts, k2tog, k1—2 sts dec'd.

Rep dec row on the next 5 (5, 6, 8, 11, 12) RS rows—70 (76, 84, 88, 92, 98) sts rem. Work even in St st until armholes measure 6 (6¼, 6¾, 7¼, 7¾, 8¼)" (15 [16, 17, 18.5, 19.5, 21] cm), ending with a WS row.

Shape Back Neck and Shoulders

With RS facing, k17 (20, 24, 20, 22, 25), BO 36 (36, 36, 48, 48, 48) sts, knit to end—17 (20, 24, 20, 22, 25) sts rem each side (see Notes). Place sts of right back neck and shoulder on holder or allow them to rest on the needle while working the left side.

Left Side

Working 17 (20, 24, 20, 22, 25) left back sts only, work 1 WS row even.

DEC ROW: (RS) K1, ssk, knit to end—1 st dec'd.

Rep the last 2 rows once more—15 (18, 22, 18, 20, 23) sts rem. Work even until armhole measures 7 (7¼, 7¾, 8¼, 8¾, 9¼)" (18 [18.5, 19.5, 21, 22, 23.5] cm), ending with a WS row. Work short-rows (see Glossary) to shape shoulder as foll:

SHORT-ROW 1: (RS) K10 (12, 14, 12, 14, 16), wrap next st, turn work.

SHORT-ROW 2: (WS) Purl to end.

SHORT-ROW 3: K5 (6, 8, 6, 6, 7), wrap next st, turn.

SHORT-ROW 4: Purl to end.

NEXT ROW: (RS) Work across all sts, working wraps tog with wrapped sts.

Place sts on holder.

Right Side

Return 17 (20, 24, 20, 22, 25) held right side sts to needle, if they are not already on the needle, and rejoin yarn with WS facing at neck edge. Work 1 WS row even.

DEC ROW: (RS) Knit to last 3 sts, k2tog, k1—1 st dec'd.

Rep the last 2 rows once more—15 (18, 22, 18, 20, 23) sts rem. Work even until armhole measures 7 (7¼, 7¾, 8¼, 8¾, 9¼)" (18 [18.5, 19.5, 21, 22, 23.5] cm), ending with a RS row. Work short-rows to shape shoulder as foll:

SHORT-ROW 1: (WS) P10 (12, 14, 12, 14, 16), wrap next st, turn work.

SHORT-ROW 2: (RS) Knit to end.

SHORT-ROW 3: P5 (6, 8, 6, 6, 7), wrap next st, turn.

SHORT-ROW 4: Knit to end.

NEXT ROW: (WS) Work across all sts, working wraps tog with wrapped sts.

Place sts on holder.

Front

Work as for back until piece measures 3¼" (8.5 cm) from CO, ending with a RS row—90 (98, 110, 122, 134, 146) sts.

SET-UP ROW: (WS) P18 (20, 22, 24, 27, 29), pm for dart, p7 (9, 13, 11, 14, 18), pm for placket, p40 (40, 40, 52, 52, 52) center sts, pm for placket, p7 (9, 13, 11, 14, 18), pm for dart, p18 (20, 22, 24, 27, 29).

DEC ROW: (RS) Knit to dart m, sl m, ssk, knit to placket m, sl m, knit center placket sts, sl m, knit to 2 sts before next dart m, k2tog, sl m, knit to end—2 sts dec'd.

[Work 7 rows even, rep dec row] 4 times—80 (88, 100, 112, 124, 136) sts rem. Work even in St st until piece measures 9½" (24 cm) from CO, ending with a WS row.

NOTE: The marked placket sts will be BO while the waist increases are in progress; read all the way through the following sections before proceeding so you do not accidentally work past the placket BO.

INC ROW: (RS) Knit to dart m, sl m, M1, knit to placket m, sl m, knit center placket sts, sl m, knit to next dart m, M1, sl m, knit to end—2 sts inc'd.

[Work 7 rows even, rep inc row] 4 times.

At the same time when piece measures 11½ (11, 11, 10¾, 10½, 10¼)" (29, 28, 28, 27.5, 26.5, 26] cm) from CO, divide right and left fronts by BO placket sts on next RS row as foll:

NEXT ROW: (RS) Work left front sts to first placket m, including waist inc if required for this row, remove placket m, BO center 40 (40, 40, 52, 52, 52) sts, remove placket m, work right front sts to end, including waist inc if required.

NOTE: The number of sts at each side depends on how many waist incs have been completed for your size at this point.

Place left front sts on holder or allow them to rest on the needle while working right front.

Right Front

Working on sts of right front only, cont as established until waist shaping has been completed—25 (29, 35, 35, 41, 47) sts rem. Work even until piece measures 15¾" (40 cm) from CO, ending with a RS row.

Tulip

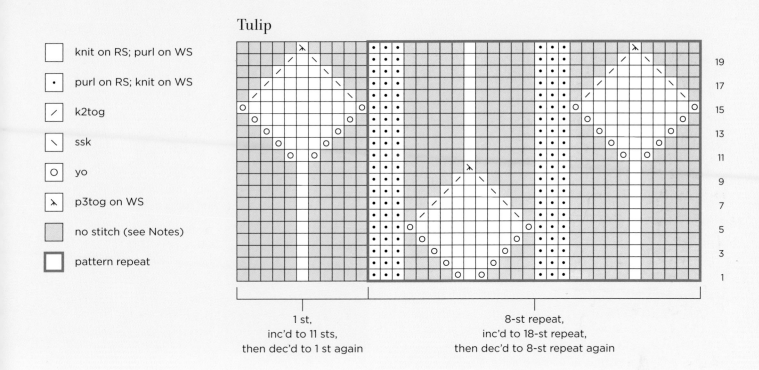

knit on RS; purl on WS

· purl on RS; knit on WS

/ k2tog

\ ssk

O yo

⅄ p3tog on WS

no stitch (see Notes)

pattern repeat

19 17 15 13 11 9 7 5 3 1

1 st,
inc'd to 11 sts,
then dec'd to 1 st again

8-st repeat,
inc'd to 18-st repeat,
then dec'd to 8-st repeat again

Shape Armhole and Shoulder

NEXT ROW: (WS) BO 4 (5, 6, 8, 9, 11) sts, purl to end—21 (24, 29, 27, 32, 36) sts rem.

DEC ROW: (RS) Knit to last 3 sts, k2tog, k1—1 st dec'd.

Rep dec row on the next 5 (5, 6, 8, 11, 12) RS rows—15 (18, 22, 18, 20, 23) sts rem. Work even until armhole measures 7 (7¼, 7¾, 8¼, 8¾, 9¼)" (18 [18.5, 19.5, 21, 22, 23.5] cm), ending with a WS row. Shape shoulder with short-rows the same as left back shoulder. Place sts on holder.

Left Front

Return held left front sts to needle, if they are not already on the needle, and join yarn with WS facing to neck edge. Work as established until waist shaping has been completed—25 (29, 35, 35, 41, 47) sts rem. Work even until piece measures 15¾" (40 cm) from CO, ending with a WS row

Shape Armhole and Shoulder

NEXT ROW: (RS) BO 4 (5, 6, 8, 9, 11) sts, knit to end—21 (24, 29, 27, 32, 36) sts rem.

Work 1 WS row even.

DEC ROW: (RS) K1, ssk, knit to end—1 st dec'd.

Rep dec row on the next 5 (5, 6, 8, 11, 12) RS rows—15 (18, 22, 18, 20, 23) sts rem. Work even until armhole measures 7 (7¼, 7¾, 8¼, 8¾, 9¼)" (18 [18.5, 19.5, 21, 22, 23.5] cm), ending with a RS row. Shape shoulder with short-rows the same as right back shoulder. Place sts on holder.

Plackets
Right Front Placket

Hold front horizontally with RS facing, lower edge of body on your right, and shoulder edge on your left. With cir needle and RS facing, join yarn to right front in corner of placket BO.

PICK-UP ROW: (RS) Pick up and purl (see Glossary) 3 (4, 3, 3, 3, 4) sts, pm, [pick up and knit 1 st, pick up and purl 3 sts] 12 (12, 14, 14, 16, 16) times, pick up and knit 1 st, pm, pick up and purl 14 (18, 14, 18, 14, 18) sts—66 (71, 74, 78, 82, 87) sts total; 49 (49, 57, 57, 65, 65) sts between m.

NEXT ROW: (WS) K14 (18, 14, 18, 14, 18) for rev St st (knit WS rows; purl RS rows), sl m, p1, [k3, p1] 12 (12, 14, 14, 16, 16] times, sl m, k3 (4, 3, 3, 3, 4) for rev St st.

NEXT ROW: (RS) Purl to m, sl m, work Row 1 of Tulip chart (page 93) over 49 (49, 57, 57, 65, 65) sts while inc as shown on chart (see Notes), sl m, purl to last 3 sts, p2tog, p1—1 st dec'd at neck edge.

NEXT ROW: (WS) K1, k2tog, knit to m, sl m, work Row 2 of chart to next m, sl m, knit to end—1 st dec'd at neck edge.

Keeping sts outside m at each side in rev St st, work Rows 3–20 of chart and *at the same time* BO 5 sts at beg of Row 4, BO 3 sts at beg of Row 6, and BO 1 st at beg of Row 8—55 (60, 63, 67, 71, 76) sts rem after completing Row 20 of chart; 3 (7, 3, 7, 3, 7) rev St sts rem at neck edge.

Sizes (42½, 46½, 50½)" only

Keeping sts at each side in rev St st, work Rows 1–10 of chart once more.

All Sizes

Work sts as they appear (knit the knits and purl the purls) for 2 rows, ending with a WS row—placket measures about 3 (3, 3, 4½, 4½, 4½)" (7.5 [7.5, 7.5, 11.5, 11.5, 11.5] cm) from pick-up row.

BUTTONHOLE ROW: (RS) P3 (6, 4, 6, 6, 5), [yo, p2tog, p4] 8 (8, 9, 9, 10, 11) times, yo, p2tog, p2 (4, 3, 5, 3, 3)—9 (9, 10, 10, 11, 12) buttonholes.

Purl 1 WS row. With RS facing, BO all sts pwise.

Left Front Placket

Hold front horizontally with RS facing, lower edge of body on your left, and shoulder edge on your right. With cir needle and RS facing, join yarn to left front at shoulder join.

PICK-UP ROW: (RS) Pick up and purl 14 (18, 14, 18, 14, 18) sts, pm, pick up and knit 1 st, [pick up and purl 3 sts, pick up and knit 1 st] 12 (12, 14, 14, 16, 16) times, pm, pick up and purl 3 (4, 3, 3, 3, 4) sts—66 (71, 74, 78, 82, 87) sts total; 49 (49, 57, 57, 65, 65) sts between m.

NEXT ROW: (WS) K3 (4, 3, 3, 3, 4) for rev St st, sl m, [p1, k3] 12 (12, 14, 14, 16, 16) times, p1, sl m, k14 (18, 14, 18, 14, 18) for rev St st.

NEXT ROW: (RS) P1, ssp (see Glossary), purl to m, sl m, work Row 1 of Tulip chart over 49 (49, 57, 57, 65, 65) sts while inc as shown on chart, sl m, purl to end—1 st dec'd at neck edge.

NEXT ROW: (WS) Knit to m, sl m, work Row 2 of chart to next m, sl m, knit to last 3 sts, ssk, k1—1 st dec'd at neck edge.

Keeping sts outside m at each side in rev St st, work Rows 3–20 of chart and *at the same time* BO 5 sts at beg of Row 3, BO 3 sts at beg of Row 5, and BO 1 st at beg of Row 7—55 (60, 63, 67, 71, 76) sts rem after completing Row 20 of chart; 3 (7, 3, 7, 3, 7) rev St sts rem at neck edge.

Sizes (42½, 46½, 50½)" only

Keeping sts at each side in rev St st, work Rows 1–10 of chart once more.

All sizes

Work sts as they appear (knit the knits and purl the purls) for 2 rows, ending with a WS row—placket measures about 3 (3, 3, 4½, 4½, 4½)" (7.5 [7.5, 7.5, 11.5, 11.5, 11.5] cm) from pick-up row. Purl 1 RS row, purl 1 WS row. With RS facing, BO all sts pwise.

Join Shoulders and Sew Sides

Block pieces to measurements. With RS facing tog and WS facing outward, use the three-needle method (see Glossary) to BO front and back shoulder sts tog at each side. With yarn threaded on a tapestry needle, sew side seams.

Sleeves

With cir needle, RS facing, and beg at shoulder join, pick up and knit 29 (30, 32, 34, 36, 38) sts evenly spaced along armhole edge to beg of underarm BO, pm, pick up and knit 8 (10, 12, 16, 18, 22) sts across underarm BO, pm, then pick up and knit 29 (30, 32, 34, 36, 38) sts evenly spaced along rem armhole edge to end at shoulder join, pm—66 (70, 76, 84, 90, 98) sts total. Work short-rows to shape cap as foll:

SHORT-ROW 1: (RS) K5, wrap next st, turn work.

SHORT-ROW 2: (WS) Purl to shoulder join m, sl m, p5, wrap next st, turn.

SHORT-ROW 3: K5, sl m, k9 working wrap tog with wrapped st, wrap next st, turn.

SHORT-ROW 4: P9, sl m, p9 working wrap tog with wrapped st, wrap next st, turn.

SHORT-ROW 5: K9, sl m, k13 working wrap tog with wrapped st, wrap next st, turn.

SHORT-ROW 6: P13, sl m, p13 working wrap tog with wrapped st, wrap next st, turn.

SHORT-ROW 7: K13, sl m, k14 working wrap tog with wrapped st, wrap next st, turn.

SHORT-ROW 8: P14, sl m, p14 working wrap tog with wrapped st, wrap next st, turn—last wrapped st at each side is the 15th st from shoulder join m.

SHORT-ROW 9: Sl m as you come to it, knit to previously wrapped st, work wrap tog with wrapped st, wrap next st, turn—wrapped st is 1 st farther from shoulder join m.

SHORT-ROW 10: Sl m as you come to it, purl to previously wrapped st, work wrap tog with wrapped st, wrap next st, turn—wrapped st is 1 st farther from shoulder join m.

Rep the last 2 rows 13 (14, 16, 18, 20, 22) more times—last wrapped st at each side is the st next to m on each side of underarm sts.

NEXT ROW: (RS) Knit to shoulder m, remove m, knit to wrapped st, work wrap tog with wrapped st, remove m, k4 (5, 6, 8, 9, 11) to center of underarm, pm for center of underarm.

NEXT RND: Change to dpn. With RS still facing, knit 1 rnd on all sts, working rem wrap tog with wrapped st, and ending at underarm m—sleeve cap measures 5 (5¼, 5¾, 6½, 7, 7½)" (12.5 [13.5, 14.5, 16.5, 18, 19] cm) from pick-up row, measured straight up along a single column of sts in center of cap. Purl 1 rnd, then knit 1 rnd. BO all sts pwise.

Finishing
Neck Edging

With cir needle, RS facing, and beg at BO edge of right front placket, pick up and knit 26 (26, 26, 31, 31, 31) sts evenly spaced along right front neck, 48 (48, 48, 60, 60, 60) sts across back neck, and 26 (26, 26, 31, 31, 31) sts evenly spaced along left front neck—100 (100, 100, 122, 122, 122) sts total. Knit 1 WS row, then knit 1 RS row. With WS facing, BO all sts kwise.

Lap last 3 rows of right front placket over corresponding rows of left front placket and sew lower edges of plackets to BO sts at base of placket opening, sewing through all three layers at the overlap.

Weave in loose ends. Sew buttons to left front placket, opposite buttonholes.

Raindrop
CARDIGAN

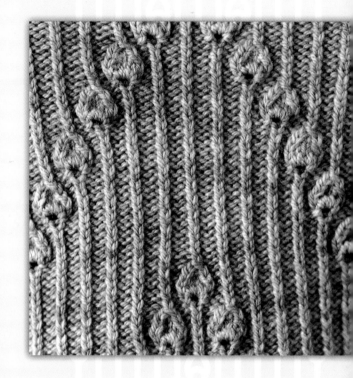

Simple twisted ribs on the fronts and a generous sailor collar make way for the dramatic bud stitch design on the back of this sporty cardigan. The body is worked in one piece to the armholes, then the fronts and back are worked separately to the shoulders. The sleeves are picked up around the armholes and then knitted down to the cuffs, leaving very little finishing once the knitting is completed. The minimally processed organic wool used here pairs nicely with the overall casual vibe.

FINISHED SIZE

About 34¼ (37¼, 41¾, 45¼, 49, 53¼)" (87 [94.5, 106, 115, 124.5, 135.5] cm) bust circumference with fronts meeting in center.

Cardigan shown measures 37¼" (94.5 cm).

yarn

DK weight (#3 Light).

SHOWN HERE: Lorna's Laces Green Line DK (100% organic merino; 145 yd [132 m]/2 oz [57 g]): echo (taupe semi-solid), 8 (9, 10, 11, 12, 12) skeins.

needles

Size U.S. 4 (3.5 mm): 24" or 32" (60 or 80 cm) circular (cir) and set of 4 or 5 double-pointed (dpn).

Adjust needle size if necessary to obtain the correct gauge.

notions

Markers (m); stitch holders; tapestry needle.

gauge

22 sts and 31 rows = 4" (10 cm) in St st.

41 to 49 sts of Willow Bud chart measure 7½" (19 cm) wide.

M5

On WS rows, work ([k1, p1] 2 times, k1) all in same st—5 sts made from 1 st.

NOTES

» The stitch count of the Willow Bud chart (page 101) varies from 41 to 49 stitches. When checking stitch counts during shaping, always count the Willow Bud panel as 41 stitches, even if the chart happens to be on a row where the stitch count has temporarily increased.

» The gray "no stitch" boxes in the chart act as placeholders where new stitches will be added or where stitches have been decreased away. When working the chart, skip over each "no stitch" symbol as you come to it; simply proceed to the next stitch.

» After working the Willow Bud chart set-up row the first time, repeat Rows 1–42 thereafter for pattern: do not repeat the set-up row.

» When working the upper back, if there are not enough rows to complete an entire willow bud motif before the neck edge, do not begin the partial motif. Instead, continue to work the stitch that would have increased for the bud as k1tbl on RS rows and as p1 on WS rows.

» Work the front edge stitches and the marked "seam" stitches as slip 1 purlwise with yarn in back (pwise wyb) on RS rows and as p1 on WS rows.

Body

With cir needle, CO 189 (205, 229, 249, 269, 293) sts. Do not join.

SET-UP ROW: (RS) Sl 1 purlwise with yarn in back (pwise wyb; edge st), [p2, k1 through back loop (tbl)] 16 (17, 19, 21, 23, 25) times, p1 (2, 2, 1, 0, 0), place marker (pm), sl 1 pwise wyb (right seam st), pm, p1 (0, 0, 1, 0, 0), k1 (0, 0, 1, 1, 1)tbl, [p2, k1tbl] 28 (31, 35, 38, 42, 46) times, p1 (2, 2, 1, 0, 0), pm, sl 1 pwise wyb (left seam st), pm, p1 (2, 2, 1, 0, 0), [k1tbl, p2] 16 (17, 19, 21, 23, 25) times, sl 1 pwise wyb (edge st)—50 (54, 60, 65, 70, 76) sts each front, 87 (95, 107, 117, 127, 139) back sts, 2 marked seam sts.

Slipping edge and seam sts (see Notes) and working RS k1tbl sts as p1 on WS rows, work in established patt for 8 more rows, ending with a RS row—piece measures ¾" (2 cm) from CO. Establish chart patt at center back as foll:

NEXT ROW: (WS) P1, [k2, p1] 5 times, k2, pm for left front band, p32 (36, 42, 47, 52, 58) left front sts, sl m, p1, sl m, p23 (27, 33, 38, 43, 49), pm, work set-up row of Willow Bud chart (page 101) over center 41 back sts inc them to 49 sts as shown on chart, pm, p23 (27, 33, 38, 43, 49), sl m, p1, sl m, p32 (36, 42, 47, 52, 58) for right front, pm for right front band, k2, [p1, k2] 5 times, p1.

NEXT ROW: (RS) Work 18 right front band sts in patt, slip marker (sl m), knit to seam st, sl m, sl 1 pwise wyb, sl m, knit to chart patt, sl m, work chart patt to next m, sl m, knit to seam st, sl m, sl 1 pwise wyb, sl m, knit to last 18 sts, sl m, work 18 left front band sts in patt.

Cont edge, seam, front band, and chart patt sts as established (see Notes), work rem sts in St st until piece measures 3¾ (3¼, 3¼, 3¼, 3¼, 3¼)" (9.5 [8.5, 8.5, 8.5, 8.5, 8.5] cm) from CO, ending with a RS row.

Shape Waist

Place dart markers (m) as foll:

With WS facing, work 18 left front band sts to m, sl m, p15 (17, 20, 23, 26, 30), pm for left front dart, p17 (19, 22, 24, 26, 28), sl m, p1, sl m, p17 (19, 22, 24, 26, 28), pm for left back dart, p6 (8, 11, 14, 17, 21), sl m, work chart patt to next m, sl m, p6 (8, 11, 14, 17, 21), pm for right back dart, p17 (19, 22, 24, 26, 28), sl m, p1, sl m, p17 (19, 22, 24, 26, 28), pm for right front dart, p15 (17, 20, 23, 26, 30), sl m, work 18 right front band sts.

DEC ROW: (RS) Keeping in established patts, work to 2 sts before right front dart m, k2tog, sl m, work to right back dart m, sl m, ssk, work to 2 sts before left back dart m, k2tog, sl m, work to left front dart m, sl m, ssk, work to end—4 sts dec'd.

[Work 7 rows even, then rep dec row] 3 times—173 (189, 213, 233, 253, 277) sts rem (see Note about counting chart sts). Work even until piece measures 9¾ (9¼, 9¼, 9¼, 9¼, 9¼)" (25 [23.5, 23.5, 23.5, 23.5, 23.5] cm) from CO, ending with a WS row.

INC ROW: (RS) Work to right front dart m, M1 (see Glossary), sl m, work to right back dart m, sl m, M1, work to left back dart m, M1, sl m, work to left front dart marker, sl m, M1, work to end—4 sts inc'd.

[Work 9 rows even, then rep dec row] 3 times—189 (205, 229, 249, 269, 293) sts. Work even in patt until piece measures 15¾ (15¼, 15¼, 15¼, 15¼, 15¼)" (40 [38.5, 38.5, 38.5, 38.5, 38.5] cm) from CO, removing dart m in first row (do not remove other m) and ending with a WS row.

Divide for Fronts and Back

NEXT ROW: (RS) Keeping in patts, work to 4 (5, 6, 8, 9, 10) sts before right seam m, BO next 9 (11, 13, 17, 19, 21) sts removing m on each side of seam st, work in patt to 4 (5, 6, 8, 9, 10) sts before left seam st, BO next 9 (11, 13, 17, 19, 21) sts removing m on each side of seam st, work in patt to end—46 (49, 54, 57, 61, 66) sts rem for each front; 79 (85, 95, 101, 109, 119) sts rem for back.

Place sts for right front and back on separate holders or allow them to rest on needle while working the left front sts.

Left Front

Working back and forth in rows on 46 (49, 54, 57, 61, 66) left front sts, work 1 WS row in patt.

DEC ROW: (RS) K1, ssk, work to end—1 st dec'd.

Rep dec row on the next 4 (5, 7, 8, 9, 11) RS rows—41 (43, 46, 48, 51, 54) sts rem. Work even as established until armhole measures 3½ (3¾, 4, 4¼, 4¼, 4½)" (9 [9.5, 10, 11, 11, 11.5] cm), ending with a WS row.

Work all sts in p2, k1tbl rib patt to match front band as foll:

With RS facing, p1 (0, 0, 0, 0, 0), k1 (1, 1, 0, 0, 0)tbl, [p2, k1tbl] 12 (13, 14, 15, 16, 17) times removing front band m as you come to it, p2, sl 1 pwise wyb.

Slipping front edge st and working all k1tbl sts as p1 on WS, cont even until armhole measures 5 (5½, 6, 6¼, 6½, 7)" (12.5 [14, 15, 16, 16.5, 18] cm), ending with a RS row.

Shape Neck

Keeping in patt, BO 18 sts at beg of next WS row, then BO 2 (2, 2, 2, 3, 3) sts at beg of next 2 WS rows, then BO 2 sts at beg of foll WS row—17 (19, 22, 24, 25, 28) sts rem.

DEC ROW: (RS) Keeping in patt, work to last 3 sts, k2tog, k1—1 st dec'd.

Work 1 WS row even, then rep the dec row once more—15 (17, 20, 22, 23, 26) sts rem. Work even until armhole measures 7 (7½, 8, 8¼, 8½, 9)" (18 [19, 20.5, 21, 21.5, 23] cm), ending with a WS row. Place sts on holder.

Right Front

Return 46 (49, 54, 57, 61, 66) held right front sts to needle, if they are not already on the needle, and join yarn with WS facing to armhole edge. Work 1 WS row even.

DEC ROW: (RS) Work in patt to last 3 sts, k2tog, k1—1 st dec'd.

Rep dec row on the next 4 (5, 7, 8, 9, 11) RS rows—41 (43, 46, 48, 51, 54) sts rem. Work even as established until armhole measures 3½ (3¾, 4, 4¼, 4¼, 4½)" (9 [9.5, 10, 11, 11, 11.5] cm), ending with a WS row.

Work all sts in p2, k1tbl rib patt to match front band as foll:

With RS facing, sl 1 pwise wyb, p2, [k1tbl, p2] 12 (13, 14, 15, 16, 17) times removing front band m as you come to it, k1 (1, 1, 0, 0, 0)tbl, p1 (0, 0, 0, 0, 0).

Slipping front edge st and working all k1tbl sts as p1 on WS, cont even until armhole measures 5 (5½, 6, 6¼, 6½, 7)" (12.5 [14, 15, 16, 16.5, 18] cm), ending with a WS row.

Shape Neck

Keeping in patt, BO 18 sts at beg of next RS row, then BO 2 (2, 2, 2, 3, 3) sts at beg of next 2 RS rows, then BO 2 sts at beg of foll RS row—17 (19, 22, 24, 25, 28) sts rem. Work 1 WS row even.

DEC ROW: (RS) K1, ssk, work in patt to end—1 st dec'd.

Work 1 WS row even, then rep the dec row once more—15 (17, 20, 22, 23, 26) sts rem. Work even until armhole measures 7 (7½, 8, 8¼, 8½, 9)" (18 [19, 20.5, 21, 21.5, 23] cm), ending with a WS row. Place sts on holder.

Back

Return 79 (85, 95, 101, 109, 119) held back sts to needle, if they are not already on the needle, and join yarn with WS facing to left armhole edge. Work 1 WS row even.

DEC ROW: (RS) K1, ssk, knit to last 3 sts, k2tog, k1—2 sts dec'd.

Rep dec row on the next 4 (5, 7, 8, 9, 11) RS rows—69 (73, 79, 83, 89, 95) sts rem. Work even until armholes measure 3½ (3¾, 4, 4¼, 4¼, 4½)" (9 [9.5, 10, 11, 11, 11.5] cm), ending with a WS row.

Work sts on each side of chart patt in p2, k1tbl rib as foll:

With RS facing, p1 (0, 0, 0, 0, 0), k1 (1, 1, 0, 0, 0)tbl, [p2, k1tbl] 4 (5, 6, 7, 8, 9) times, sl m, work chart patt to next m, sl m, [k1tbl, p2] 4 (5, 6, 7, 8, 9) times, k1 (1, 1, 0, 0, 0)tbl, p1 (0, 0, 0, 0, 0).

Working chart patt as established and working all k1tbl sts as p1 on WS rows, cont even until armholes measure 7 (7½, 8, 8¼, 8½, 9)" (18 [19, 20.5, 21, 21.5, 23] cm), ending with a WS row (see Notes).

NEXT ROW: (RS) Work 15 (17, 20, 22, 23, 26) sts in patt, BO center sts until 14 (16, 19, 21, 22, 25) sts rem on left needle (1 st on right needle after last BO), work in patt to end—15 (17, 20, 22, 23, 26) sts rem at each side.

Place sts on separate holders for shoulders.

Join Shoulders

Block body to measurements. With RS touching and WS facing outward, use the three-needle method (see Glossary) to BO 15 (17, 20, 22, 23, 26) front and back shoulder sts tog at each side.

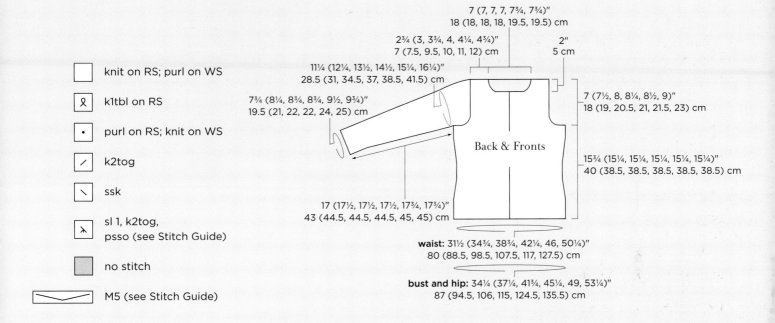

- knit on RS; purl on WS
- k1tbl on RS
- purl on RS; knit on WS
- k2tog
- ssk
- sl 1, k2tog, psso (see Stitch Guide)
- no stitch
- M5 (see Stitch Guide)

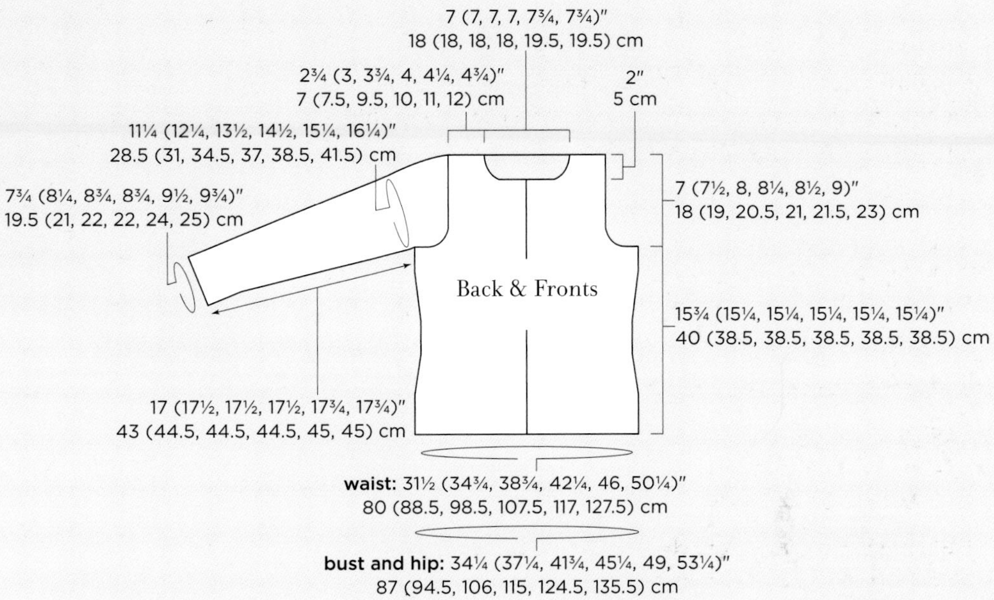

7 (7, 7, 7, 7¾, 7¾)"
18 (18, 18, 18, 19.5, 19.5) cm
2¾ (3, 3¾, 4, 4¼, 4¾)"
7 (7.5, 9.5, 10, 11, 12) cm
2"
5 cm
11¼ (12¼, 13½, 14½, 15¼, 16¼)"
28.5 (31, 34.5, 37, 38.5, 41.5) cm
7¾ (8¼, 8¾, 8¾, 9½, 9¾)"
19.5 (21, 22, 22, 24, 25) cm
7 (7½, 8, 8¼, 8½, 9)"
18 (19, 20.5, 21, 21.5, 23) cm
Back & Fronts
15¾ (15¼, 15¼, 15¼, 15¼, 15¼)"
40 (38.5, 38.5, 38.5, 38.5, 38.5) cm
17 (17½, 17½, 17½, 17¾, 17¾)"
43 (44.5, 44.5, 44.5, 45, 45) cm
waist: 31½ (34¾, 38¾, 42¼, 46, 50¼)"
80 (88.5, 98.5, 107.5, 117, 127.5) cm
bust and hip: 34¼ (37¼, 41¾, 45¼, 49, 53¼)"
87 (94.5, 106, 115, 124.5, 135.5) cm

Willow Bud

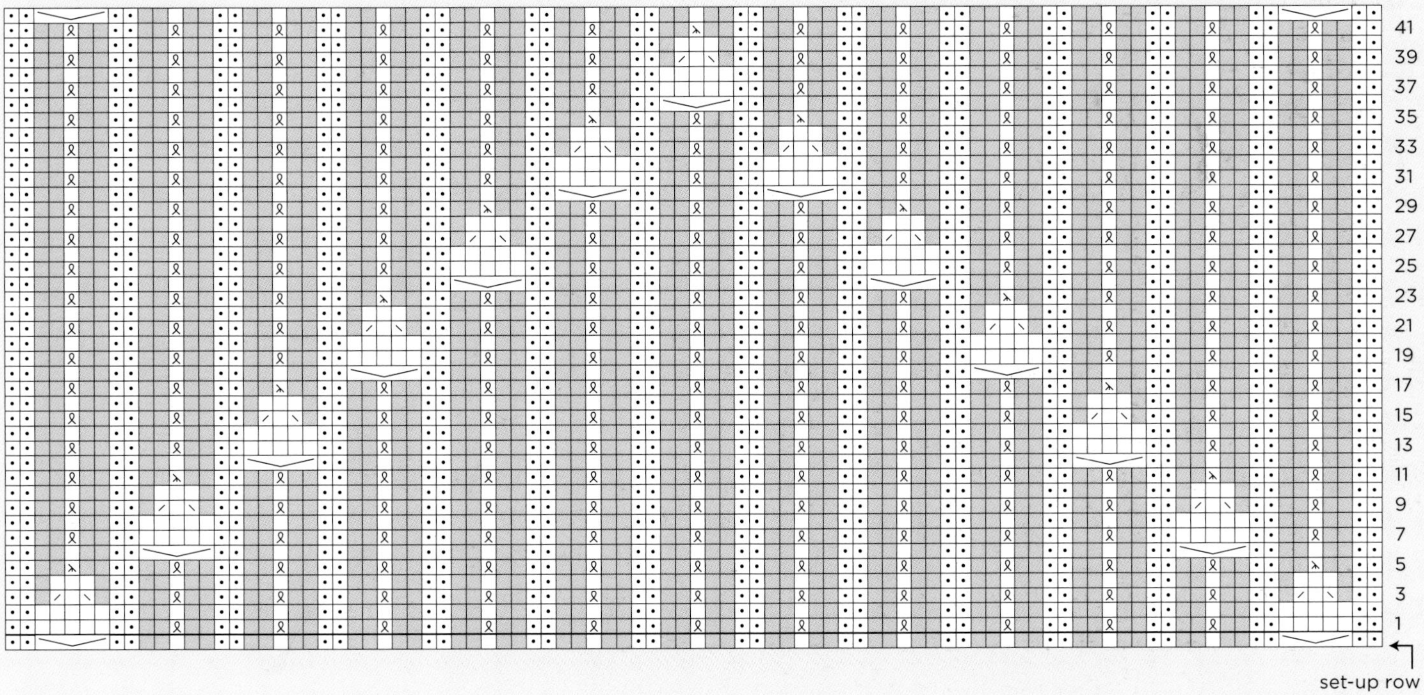

41
39
37
35
33
31
29
27
25
23
21
19
17
15
13
11
9
7
5
3
1
set-up row

Sleeves

With cir needle, RS facing, and beg at shoulder join, pick up and knit 27 (29, 31, 32, 33, 35) sts evenly spaced (about 1 st for every 2 rows) to underarm BO, pm, 8 (10, 12, 16, 18, 20) sts across underarm BO, pm, then 27 (29, 31, 32, 33, 35) sts along rem armhole edge to end at shoulder join, pm—62 (68, 74, 80, 84, 90) sts total.

Cap

Work short-rows to shape cap as foll:

SHORT-ROW 1: (RS) K5, wrap next st, turn work.

SHORT-ROW 2: (WS) Purl to shoulder join m, sl m, p5, wrap next st, turn.

SHORT-ROW 3: K5, sl m, k10 working wrap tog with wrapped st, wrap next st, turn.

SHORT-ROW 4: P10, sl m, p10 working wrap tog with wrapped st, wrap next st, turn.

SHORT-ROW 5: K10, sl m, k11 working wrap tog with wrapped st, wrap next st, turn.

SHORT-ROW 6: P11, sl m, p11 working wrap tog with wrapped st, wrap next st, turn—last wrapped st at each side is the 12th st from shoulder join m.

SHORT-ROW 7: Sl m as you come to it, knit to previously wrapped st, work wrap tog with wrapped st, wrap next st, turn—wrapped st is 1 st farther from shoulder join m.

SHORT-ROW 8: Sl m as you come to it, purl to previously wrapped st, work wrap tog with wrapped st, wrap next st, turn—wrapped st is 1 st farther from shoulder join m.

Rep the last 2 rows 14 (16, 18, 19, 20, 22) more times—last wrapped st at each side is the st next to m on each side of underarm sts.

NEXT ROW: (RS) Knit to shoulder m, remove m, knit to wrapped st, work wrap tog with wrapped st, remove m, k4 (5, 6, 8, 9, 10) to center of underarm, pm for center of underarm.

NEXT RND: (WS) Change to dpn. With RS still facing, knit 1 rnd on all sts, working rem wrap tog with wrapped st and

ending at underarm m—sleeve cap measures 5 (5½, 6, 6¼, 6½, 7)" (12.5 [14, 15, 16, 16.5, 18] cm) from pick-up row, measured straight up along a single column of sts in center of cap.

Lower Sleeve

Knit 4 rnds even.

DEC RND: K1, ssk, knit to last 3 sts, k2tog, k1—2 sts dec'd.

[Work 9 (9, 7, 6, 6, 5) rnds even, then rep dec rnd] 9 (10, 12, 15, 15, 17) times—42 (46, 48, 48, 52, 54) sts rem. Work even until sleeve measures 14 (14½, 14½, 14½, 14¾, 14¾)" (35.5 [37, 37, 37, 37.5, 37.5] cm) from joining rnd.

NEXT RND: [K1tbl, p2] 14 (15, 16, 16, 17, 18) times, k0 (1, 0, 0, 1, 0) tbl.

NEXT RND: [K1, p2] 14 (15, 16, 16, 17, 18), k0 (1, 0, 0, 1, 0).

Rep the last 2 rnds until sleeve measures 17 (17½, 17½, 17½, 17¾, 17¾)" (43 [44.5, 44.5, 44.5, 45, 45] cm) from joining rnd. BO all sts in rib patt.

Finishing

Collar

NOTE: The RS of the collar corresponds to the WS of the garment so the RS of the collar's rib patt will show on the outside when the collar is folded down.

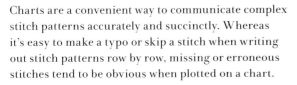

Charts are a convenient way to communicate complex stitch patterns accurately and succinctly. Whereas it's easy to make a typo or skip a stitch when writing out stitch patterns row by row, missing or erroneous stitches tend to be obvious when plotted on a chart.

For the Raindrop Cardigan, the staggered willow bud pattern consists of 41 stitches that repeat over 42 rows. To complicate matters, the number of stitches changes from one row to another. Written out in rows, this stitch pattern would be needlessly complicated and would lack an intuitive structure. But when presented in a chart (page 101), a clear pattern of stockinette buds against a k1, p2 background emerges. At a glance, you can see how the decreases, increases, knits, and purls relate to each other.

Like all types of shorthand, knitting charts follow a simple set of rules—each square represents a stitch and a predetermined set of symbols is used to indicate how each stitch should be worked. Unless otherwise specified, charts are read from bottom to top, right-side rows are read from right to left, and wrong-side rows are read from left to right. For patterns worked in the round in which the right side is always facing the knitter, all rows of the chart are read from right to left. Row numbers on charts are typically positioned to indicate the starting point of each row/round.

Stitch patterns involve two types of repeats—horizontal stitch repeats and vertical row repeats—that represent the smallest unique unit of the pattern. A single repeat in a chart is typically outlined in red. Iterations of this unique unit are worked to make a larger pattern. For the Raindrop Cardigan, the 41 stitches of the willow bud pattern are worked only once across the width of the back, but the 42 rows of the pattern are repeated several times along the length.

Typically, the number of stitches in a pattern repeat remains constant from row to row. However, the stitch count changes over the course of a vertical repeat of the willow bud pattern used in the Raindrop Cardigan. Shaded "no-stitch" symbols are therefore used to keep the stitches in the chart aligned vertically as they will appear in the knitting. For this type of chart, simply skip over the "no-stitch" symbols as you come to them. Note that although the stitch count may change from row to row, the last row of a repeat will have the same number of stitches as the first row. This ensures that the resulting fabric will lie flat without puckers.

Of course, there are times when puckers or scallops are warranted, especially at the edges or hems of garments, as for the hem in the Tulip Henley (page 88). These types of stitch patterns usually involve casting on excess stitches and then decreasing to the desired width or, conversely, increasing stitches just before binding off.

With cir needle and WS of garment facing, pick up and knit 35 (35, 35, 35, 36, 36) sts along left front neck edge, 39 (39, 39, 39, 43, 43) sts across back neck, and 35 (35, 35, 35, 36, 36) sts along right front neck edge—109 (109, 109, 109, 115, 115) sts total.

SET-UP ROW: (WS of collar; RS of garment) P1, *k2, p1; rep from * to end.

NEXT ROW: (RS of collar; WS of garment) Sl 1 pwise wyb, *p2, k1tbl; rep from * to last 3 sts, p2, sl 1 pwise wyb.

Rep the last 2 rows until collar measures 4¾" (12 cm) or desired length from pick-up row. BO all sts in rib patt.

Weave in loose ends. Block again, if desired.

Cecily PULLOVER

Staggered ribs at the yoke are echoed across the hipline and again near the hem of this raglan pullover. Falling just past the hips and worked in a soft heathery tweed, this gently fitted silhouette exudes casual ease. Because it is worked from the top down, you can try on the piece and make adjustments to the body and sleeve length along the way. Gentle waist shaping along princess seams provides subtle shape, while generous sleeves and front pockets complete the relaxed look.

FINISHED SIZE

About 32 (34½, 38¼, 41¾, 45, 48¾, 52¼)" (81.5 [87.5, 97, 106, 114.5, 124, 132.5] cm) bust circumference.

Pullover shown measures 34½" (87.5 cm).

yarn
Worsted weight (#4 Medium).

SHOWN HERE: Classic Elite Yarns Portland Tweed (50% virgin wool, 25% alpaca; 25% viscose; 120 yd [109 m]/50 g): #5054 barely there lilac, 8 (9, 9, 10, 11, 12, 12) skeins.

needles
BODY AND SLEEVES: size U.S. 7 (4.5 mm): 24" (60 cm) circular (cir) and set of 4 or 5 double-pointed (dpn).

POCKET LININGS: size U.S. 6 (4 mm).

Adjust needle size if necessary to obtain the correct gauge.

notions
Markers (m; one in a unique color); cable needle (cn); waste yarn for holding stitches; tapestry needle.

gauge
19 sts and 27 rnds = 4" (10 cm) in St st on larger needle, worked in rnds.

stitch guide

LT (left twist)

Sl 1 st onto cable needle (cn) and hold in front of work, k1, k1 from cn.

Yoke

With larger cir needle, CO 108 (112, 114, 114, 114, 116, 116) sts. Place marker (pm) of unique color and join for working in rnds, being careful not to twist sts.

SET-UP RND: K16 for right sleeve, pm, k38 (40, 41, 41, 41, 42, 42) for front, pm, k16 for left sleeve, pm, k38 (40, 41, 41, 41, 42, 42) for back—rnd begins at right back raglan m.

INC RND: *K1 (raglan st), M1 (see Glossary), knit to 1 st before next m, M1, k1 (raglan st), slip marker (sl m); rep from * 3 more times—8 sts inc'd.

NEXT RND: Knit.

Rep the last 2 rnds 2 (3, 4, 5, 5, 6, 6) more times, then work the inc rnd once more—140 (152, 162, 170, 170, 180, 180) sts total; 24 (26, 28, 30, 30, 32, 32) sts each sleeve; 46 (50, 53, 55, 55, 58, 58) sts each for front and back; piece measures 1¼ (1½, 1¾, 2, 2, 2¼, 2¼)" (3.2 [3.8, 4.5, 5, 5, 5.5, 5.5] cm) from CO.

NOTE: Measure yoke length straight up along a single column of sts; do not measure along the diagonal raglan lines.

Yoke Texture Pattern

Established textured patt according to your size on next rnd as foll.

Sizes 32 (48¾, 52¼)"

RND 1: *K1 (raglan st), [k2, p2] 5 (7, 7) times, k2, k1 (raglan st), sl m, k1 (raglan st), p1, [k2, p2] 10 (13, 13) times, k2, p1, k1 (raglan st), sl m; rep from * once more.

Size 34½"

RND 1: *K1 (raglan st), k1, p2, [k2, p2] 5 times, k1, k1 (raglan st), sl m, k1 (raglan st), k1, p2, [k2, p2] 11 times, k1, k1 (raglan st), sl m; rep from * once more.

Size 38¼"

RND 1: *K1 (raglan st), [k2, p2] 6 times, k2, k1 (raglan st), sl m, k1 (raglan st), [k2, p2] 12 times, k2, p1, k1 (raglan st), sl m; rep from * once more.

Sizes (41¾, 45)"

RND 1: *K1 (raglan st), k1, p2, [k2, p2] 6 times, k1, k1 (raglan st), sl m, k1 (raglan st), p1, [k2, p2] 13 times, k1 (raglan st), sl m; rep from * once more.

All sizes

RND 2: *K1, M1, work in established k2, p2 rib to 1 st before next m, M1, k1, sl m; rep from * 3 more times—8 sts inc'd.

RND 3: *K1, work in established k2, p2 rib patt to 1 st before next m while working new sts into patt, k1, sl m; rep from * 3 more times.

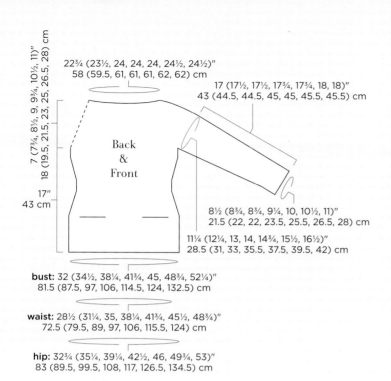

22¾ (23½, 24, 24, 24, 24½, 24½)"
58 (59.5, 61, 61, 61, 62, 62) cm

17 (17½, 17½, 17¾, 17¾, 18, 18)"
43 (44.5, 44.5, 45, 45, 45.5, 45.5) cm

7 (7¾, 8½, 9, 9¾, 10½, 11)"
18 (19.5, 21.5, 23, 25, 26.5, 28) cm

Back & Front

17"
43 cm

8½ (8¾, 8¾, 9¼, 10, 10½, 11)"
21.5 (22, 22, 23.5, 25.5, 26.5, 28) cm

11¼ (12¼, 13, 14, 14¾, 15½, 16½)"
28.5 (31, 33, 35.5, 37.5, 39.5, 42) cm

bust: 32 (34½, 38¼, 41¾, 45, 48¾, 52¼)"
81.5 (87.5, 97, 106, 114.5, 124, 132.5) cm

waist: 28½ (31¼, 35, 38¼, 41¾, 45½, 48¾)"
72.5 (79.5, 89, 97, 106, 115.5, 124) cm

hip: 32¾ (35¼, 39¼, 42½, 46, 49¾, 53)"
83 (89.5, 99.5, 108, 117, 126.5, 134.5) cm

RNDS 4 AND 5: Rep Rnds 2 and 3—156 (168, 178, 186, 186, 196, 196) sts total; 28 (30, 32, 34, 34, 36, 36) sts each sleeve; 50 (54, 57, 59, 59, 62, 62) sts each for front and back.

RND 6: Working a LT (see Stitch Guide) over the sts of each complete 2-st knit or purl column, and working any single k1 or p1 sts of the rib patt as they appear, *k1, M1, work in patt with LT's to 1 st before next m, M1, k1, sl m; rep from * 3 more times—8 sts inc'd.

RND 7: Reversing the rib patt established on Rnds 1–5 by purling the previous knit sts and knitting the previous purl sts, *k1, work in reversed k2, p2 rib patt to 1 st before next m while working new sts into new reversed rib patt, k1, sl m; rep from * 3 more times.

RND 8: *K1, M1, work in rib patt to 1 st before next m, M1, k1, sl m; rep from * 3 more times—8 sts inc'd.

RND 9: *K1, work in rib patt to next m while working new sts into patt, k1, sl m; rep from * 3 more times.

RNDS 10-13: Rep Rnds 8 and 9 two more times—188 (200, 210, 218, 218, 228, 228) sts total; 36 (38, 40, 42, 42, 44, 44) sts each sleeve; 58 (62, 65, 67, 67, 70, 70) sts each for front and back.

Cont for your size as foll.

Sizes 32 (34½)"

Skip to All Sizes.

Sizes (38¼, 41¾, 45, 48¾, 52¼)"

NEXT RND: *K1, M1, knit to 1 st before next m, M1, k1; rep from * 3 more times—8 sts inc'd.

NEXT RND: Knit.

Rep the last 2 rnds (1, 3, 5, 7, 10) more time(s)—(226, 250, 266, 292, 316) sts total; (44, 50, 54, 60, 66) sts each sleeve; (69, 75, 79, 86, 92) sts each for front and back.

All sizes

Cont in St st, work 2 rnds even—3 rnds worked even since previous inc rnd for all sizes. [Work inc rnd, then work 3 rnds even] 6 (7, 6, 5, 5, 4, 3) times—236 (256, 274, 290, 306, 324, 340) sts total; 48 (52, 56, 60, 64, 68, 72) sts each sleeve; 70 (76, 81, 85, 89, 94, 98) sts each for front and back; piece measures about 7 (7¾, 8, 8¼, 9, 9¼, 9½)" (18 [19.5, 20.5, 21, 23, 23.5, 24] cm) from CO. Cont according to your size as foll:

Sizes 32 (34½)"

Yoke is complete; skip to Divide for Body and Sleeves.

Sizes (38¼, 41¾, 45, 48¾, 52¼)"

NEXT RND: *Knit across sleeve sts to next m, sl m, k1, M1, knit to 1 st before next m, M1, k1, sl m; rep from * once more—4 sts inc'd; 2 sts each on front and back; no change to sleeve sts.

Rep the last rnd every rnd (1, 3, 5, 7, 9) more time(s)—(282, 306, 330, 356, 380) sts total; (56, 60, 64, 68, 72) sts each sleeve; (85, 93, 101, 110, 118) sts each for front and back; piece measures (8½, 9, 9¾, 10½, 11)" ([21.5, 23, 25, 26.5, 28] cm) from CO.

Divide for Body and Sleeves

Remove raglan m as you come to them and place new m as foll: *Place 48 (52, 56, 60, 64, 68, 72) right sleeve sts on waste yarn holder, use the backward-loop method (see Glossary) to CO 3 sts for half of right underarm, pm for right side "seam," CO 3 sts for other half of right underarm; k12 (14, 15, 17, 18, 20, 22) front sts, pm for right front dart, k46 (48, 55, 59, 65, 70, 74) center front sts, pm for left front dart, k12 (14, 15, 17, 18, 20, 22) left front sts; rep from * for left sleeve, left underarm, and back, then knit the first 3 CO sts again, pm for beg of rnd in center of underarm, and rejoin for knitting in rnds—152 (164, 182, 198, 214, 232, 248) sts total; 76 (82, 91, 99, 107, 116, 124) sts each for front and back; rnd beg at right side at start of front sts.

Body

Knit 10 rnds—piece measures 1½" (3.8 cm) from dividing rnd.

DEC RND: *Knit to dart m, sl m, ssk, work to 2 sts before next dart m, k2tog, sl m, knit to side m, sl m; rep from * once more—4 sts dec'd; 2 sts each from front and back.

[Work 7 rnds even, then rep the dec rnd] 3 times—136 (148, 166, 182, 198, 216, 232) sts rem; piece measures 5¼" (13.5 cm) from dividing rnd. Work even until lower body measures 7 (7, 7, 6½, 6¼, 6, 5¾)" (18 [18, 18, 16.5, 16, 15, 14.5] cm) from dividing rnd and entire piece measures about 14 (14¾, 15½, 15½, 16, 16½, 16¾)" (35.5 [37.5, 39.5, 39.5, 40.5, 42, 42.5] cm) from initial CO.

INC RND: *Knit to dart m, sl m, M1, knit to next dart m, M1, sl m, knit to side m, sl m; rep from * once more—4 sts inc'd; 2 sts each for front and back.

[Work 5 rnds even, then rep the inc rnd] 4 more times—156 (168, 186, 202, 218, 236, 252) sts; 78 (84, 93, 101, 109, 118, 126) sts each for front and back; piece measures 10¾ (10¾, 10¾, 10¼, 10, 9¾, 9½)" (27.5 [27.5, 27.5, 26, 25.5, 25, 24] cm) from dividing rnd. Removing dart m in next rnd while leaving side m in place, work even in St st until piece measures 11" (28 cm) from dividing rnd for all sizes.

Pocket Openings

POCKET SET-UP RND: K6 (9, 10, 10, 12, 12, 12), sl next 20 (20, 20, 20, 22, 22, 22) sts onto waste yarn holder without knitting them, use the backward-loop method to CO 20 (20, 20, 20, 22, 22, 22) sts over gap, k26 (26, 33, 41, 41, 50, 58) center front sts, sl next 20 (20, 20, 20, 22, 22, 22) sts onto waste yarn holder without knitting them, CO 20 (20, 20, 20, 22, 22, 22) sts over gap as before, k6 (9, 10, 10, 12, 12, 12), sl m, knit across back sts to end.

Lower Body

Work 7 rnds in textured patt as foll:

RNDS 1–6: *P2 (1, 2, 2, 1, 2, 2), [k2, p2] 19 (20, 22, 24, 27, 29, 31) times, k0 (2, 2, 2, 0, 0, 0), p0 (1, 1, 1, 0, 0, 0), sl m; rep from * once more.

RND 7: *P0 (1, 0, 0, 1, 0, 0), [LT] 39 (41, 46, 50, 54, 59, 63) times, p0 (1, 1, 1, 0, 0, 0), sl m; rep from * once more—piece measures 12″ (30.5 cm) from dividing rnd and 1″ (2.5 cm) from pocket set-up rnd.

Work even in St st for 3″ (7.5 cm)—piece measures 15″ (38 cm) from dividing rnd and 4″ (10 cm) from pocket set-up rnd. Work Rnds 1–7 of lower body textured patt once more, then work even in St st for 1″ (2.5 cm) after last patt rnd—piece measures 17″ (43 cm) from dividing rnd. Loosely BO all sts.

Sleeves

Place 48 (52, 56, 60, 64, 68, 72) held sleeve sts on larger dpn. With RS facing, join yarn to end of sleeve sts, pick up and knit 3 sts along first half of sts CO at underarm, pm, then pick up and knit 3 sts along second half of underarm CO—54 (58, 62, 66, 70, 74, 78) sts total. Knit 3 rnds even, ending each rnd at m in center of underarm.

DEC RND: Ssk, knit to 2 sts before m, k2tog—2 sts dec'd.

[Work 13 (13, 9, 8, 8, 8, 7) rnds even, then rep the dec rnd] 6 (7, 9, 10, 10, 11, 12) more times—40 (42, 42, 44, 48, 50, 52) sts rem. Work even in St st until sleeve measures 17 (17½, 17½, 17¾, 17¾, 18, 18)″ (43 [44.5, 44.5, 45, 45, 45.5, 45.5] cm).

Loosely BO all sts.

Finishing

Block to measurements.

Neck Edging

With cir needle and RS facing, pick up and knit 108 (112, 114, 114, 114, 116, 116) sts evenly spaced around neck opening. Do not join. Knit 1 WS row, then BO all sts kwise with RS facing. With yarn threaded on a tapestry needle, sew selvedges tog.

Lower Edging

With cir needle and RS facing, pick up and knit 156 (168, 186, 202, 218, 236, 252) sts evenly spaced around lower edge. Do not join. Knit 1 WS row, then BO all sts kwise with RS facing. Sew selvedges tog.

Cuff Edging

With dpn and RS facing, pick up and knit 40 (42, 42, 44, 48, 50, 52) sts evenly spaced around cuff edge. Do not join. Knit 1 WS row, then BO all sts kwise with RS facing. Sew selvedges tog.

Pocket Linings

Hold garment upside-down. Place 20 (20, 20, 20, 22, 22, 22) held pocket sts on smaller needles and join yarn with RS facing. Work even in St st for 5″ (12.5 cm), or until lining reaches Rnd 7 of the last textured patt band, ending with a RS row. With WS of garment facing, mark the 20 (20, 20, 20, 22, 22, 22) sts directly below the pocket opening in the first rnd after last textured patt rnd and, with WS facing, sl an empty dpn into the 20 (20, 20, 20, 22, 22, 22) purl bumps of the marked sts without working any sts. Hold dpn with picked-up sts and pocket lining needle tog with WS of lining facing you and lining needle in front. BO sts tog to close bottom of pocket as foll: K2tog (1 st from each needle), *k2tog (1 st from each needle), pass first st on right-hand needle over the second st to BO; rep from * until all live pocket lining sts have been BO. With yarn threaded on a tapestry needle, sew sides of pocket linings to WS of body.

Weave in loose ends.

Intagliata
HENLEY

Panels of nested diamonds, pretty ribs, and columns of bamboo stitch take center stage in this classic Henley. Worked in a fine yarn for a slim silhouette, this comfortable trans-seasonal garment includes such sophisticated details as side slits, a neckline notch, and three-quarter-length sleeves. The ribbings in the collar, cuffs, and at the lower edge echo the pattern in the placket. Surprisingly easy to knit, this piece requires a minimum amount of seaming—the body is worked in the round to the armholes and the sleeves are worked in the round from the top down.

FINISHED SIZE

34 (37¼, 41¼, 44¾, 48¾, 52)" (86.5 [94, 105, 113.5, 124, 132] cm) bust circumference.

Sweater shown measures 34" (86.5 cm).

yarn

Fingering weight (#1 Super Fine).

SHOWN HERE: Madelinetosh Tosh Sock (100% merino; 395 yd [361 m]/4 oz [114 g]): nutmeg, 3 (4, 4, 4, 5, 5) skeins.

needles

U.S. size 4 (3.5 mm): 24" (60 cm) circular (cir) and set of 4 or 5 double-pointed (dpn).

Adjust needle size if necessary to obtain the correct gauge.

notions

Waste yarn for holding stitches; cable needle (cn); markers (m); stitch holders; tapestry needle.

gauge

24 sts and 36 rows = 4" (10 cm) in St st.

52 (64) sts of Center Panel chart measure 7¾ (9½)" (19.5 [24] cm) wide.

stitch guide

Yo-k2-pass

Yo, k2, pass yo over 2 knit sts.

NOTES

» The center panel represents 52 stitches for the four smallest sizes and 64 stitches for the two largest sizes. The stitches shaded in gray are worked for the two largest sizes only.

» For each row or round of the four smallest sizes, work the 9 chart stitches before the first shaded section, skip the 6 shaded stitches, work the center 34 stitches, skip the next 6 shaded stitches, then work the last 9 stitches of the chart. For the two largest sizes, work across all 64 stitches of the entire chart.

» The set-up round of the center panel chart is worked only once. After working the set-up round to establish the pattern, repeat Rows/Rnds 1–16 of the chart thereafter: do not repeat the set-up round.

Body

Side Slits

With cir needle, CO 112 (124, 136, 148, 160, 172) sts. Do not join.

NEXT ROW: (RS) *K1, p2; rep from * to last st, k1.

Working back and forth in rows, work sts as they appear (knit the knits and purl the purls) until piece measures 1" (2.5 cm) from CO, ending with a WS row. Break yarn and place sts on waste yarn holder. Work a second piece in the same manner, but leave sts on needle and do not break yarn. Return sts of held piece to end of needle with RS facing; sts of piece with working yarn attached will be worked first on next rnd.

JOINING RND: Bring ends of needle tog for working in the rnd, sl last st of second piece from end of right-hand needle to beg of left-hand needle, place marker (pm) on left-hand needle for beg of rnd. Slip marker (sl m), k2tog (transferred st from second piece tog with first st of first piece), *p2, k1, p2, k0 (1, 2, 3, 2, 5), [k9 (8, 9, 8, 9, 8), k2tog] 9 (11, 11, 13, 13, 15) times, k1 (1, 1, 3, 3, 5), p2, k1, p2,* pm for right side, k2tog (last st of first piece tog with first st of second piece); rep from * to * once more—204 (224, 248, 268, 292, 312) sts total; rnd begins at left side, at start of front sts.

Lower Body

NEXT RND: *[K1, p2] 2 times, knit to 5 sts before side m, p2, k1, p2; rep from * once more.

Rep the last rnd until piece measures 2" (5 cm) from CO.

NEXT RND: *P1 for "seam," pm, k101 (111, 123, 133, 145, 155), sl m; rep from * once more.

Purling the seam sts every rnd, work in St st until piece measures 4½" (11.5 cm) from CO.

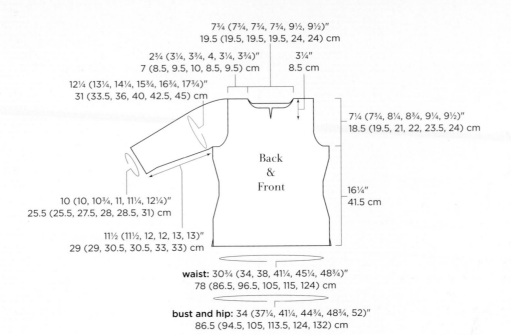

7¾ (7¾, 7¾, 7¾, 9½, 9½)"
19.5 (19.5, 19.5, 19.5, 24, 24) cm

2¾ (3¼, 3¾, 4, 3¼, 3¾)"
7 (8.5, 9.5, 10, 8.5, 9.5) cm

3¼"
8.5 cm

12¼ (13¼, 14¼, 15¾, 16¾, 17¾)"
31 (33.5, 36, 40, 42.5, 45) cm

7¼ (7¾, 8¼, 8¾, 9¼, 9½)"
18.5 (19.5, 21, 22, 23.5, 24) cm

Back & Front

16¼"
41.5 cm

10 (10, 10¾, 11, 11¼, 12¼)"
25.5 (25.5, 27.5, 28, 28.5, 31) cm

11½ (11½, 12, 12, 13, 13)"
29 (29, 30.5, 30.5, 33, 33) cm

waist: 30¾ (34, 38, 41¼, 45¼, 48¾)"
78 (86.5, 96.5, 105, 115, 124) cm

bust and hip: 34 (37¼, 41¼, 44¾, 48¾, 52)"
86.5 (94.5, 105, 113.5, 124, 132) cm

Shape Waist

NEXT RND: *P1, sl m, k27 (29, 32, 35, 38, 41), pm for dart, k47 (53, 59, 63, 69, 73), pm for dart, k27 (29, 32, 35, 38, 41), sl m; rep from * once more.

DEC RND: *P1, sl m, knit to dart m, sl m, ssk, knit to 2 sts before next dart m, k2tog, sl m, knit to seam st, sl m; rep from * once more—4 sts dec'd.

[Work 7 rnds even, then rep the dec row] 4 times—184 (204, 228, 248, 272, 292) sts rem; piece measures about 8¼" (21 cm) from CO. Work even until piece measures 10½" (26.5 cm) from CO.

INC RND: *P1, sl m, knit to dart m, sl m, M1 (see Glossary), work to next dart m, M1, sl m, knit to seam st, sl m; rep from * once more—4 sts inc'd.

[Work 7 rnds even, the rep the inc rnd] 4 times—204 (224, 248, 268, 292, 312) sts. Work 1 rnd even, removing dart m on next rnd, leaving end-of-rnd and seam markers in place—piece measures 14¼" (36 cm) from CO. Work even if necessary for your size until piece measures 14¾" (37.5 cm) from CO for all sizes.

Front Center Panel

INC RND: P1, sl m, k27 (32, 38, 43, 44, 49), pm, k1, [k9 (9, 9, 9, 8, 8), M1] 5 (5, 5, 5, 7, 7) times, k1 (1, 1, 1, 0, 0), pm, k27 (32, 38, 43, 44, 49), sl m, p1, sl m, knit to end—209 (229, 253, 273, 299, 319) sts; 107 (117, 129, 139, 153, 163) front sts; 102 (112, 124, 134, 146, 156) back sts; 52 (52, 52, 52, 64, 64) sts between new m at center front.

NEXT RND: P1, sl m, knit to next m, sl m, work set-up rnd of Center Panel chart (page 115) over 52 (52, 52, 52, 64, 64) marked center front sts (see Notes), sl m, knit to seam st, sl m, p1, sl m, knit to end.

Cont in patts as established (see Notes) until piece measures 16¼" (41.5 cm] from CO for all sizes, ending last rnd 5 (6, 7, 9, 10, 12) sts before end-of-rnd m at left side.

Divide for Front and Back

NEXT RND: BO last 5 (6, 7, 9, 10, 12) sts of previous rnd for half of left armhole, remove end-of-rnd m, BO first 6 (7, 8, 10, 11, 13) sts of next rnd for other half of left armhole, work in patt to 5 (6, 7, 9, 10, 12) sts before right side seam st, BO 11 (13, 15, 19, 21, 25) sts for right armhole removing seam st markers as you come to them, knit to end—91 (99, 109, 115, 125, 131) back sts; 96 (104, 114, 120, 132, 138) front sts. Place front sts on holder.

Upper Back

Working back and forth in rows on 91 (99, 109, 115, 125, 131) back sts only, purl 1 WS row.

Shape Armholes

DEC ROW: (RS) K1, ssk, knit to last 3 sts, k2tog, k1—2 sts dec'd.

[Work 1 WS row even, then rep the dec row] 4 (6, 8, 9, 13, 13) times—81 (85, 91, 95, 97, 103) sts rem. Work even until armholes measure 6½ (7, 7½, 8, 8½, 8¾)" (16.5 [18, 19, 20.5, 21.5, 22] cm), ending with a WS row.

Shape Left Back Neck

NEXT ROW: (RS) K18 (20, 23, 25, 21, 24), BO 45 (45, 45, 45, 55, 55) sts, knit to end—18 (20, 23, 25, 21, 24) sts rem each side.

Place sts of right back neck on holder or allow them to rest on needle while working the left back neck.

NOTE: The two largest sizes deliberately have fewer shoulder sts because the back neck widths correspond to the width of the center panel patterns on the front.

Working sts of left back neck only, work 1 WS row even.

DEC ROW: (RS) K1, ssk, knit to end—17 (19, 22, 24, 20, 23) sts rem.

Work even until armhole measures 7¼ (7¾, 8¼, 8¾, 9¼, 9½)" (18.5 [19.5, 21, 22, 23.5, 24] cm), ending with a WS row. Place sts on holder.

Shape Right Back Neck

Return 18 (20, 23, 25, 21, 24) held right back neck sts to needle, if they are not already on the needle, and rejoin yarn with WS facing at neck edge. Work 1 WS row even in patt.

DEC ROW: (RS) Knit to last 3 sts, k2tog, k1—17 (19, 22, 24, 20, 23) sts rem.

Work even until armhole measures 7¼ (7¾, 8¼, 8¾, 9¼, 9½)" (18.5 [19.5, 21, 22, 23.5, 24] cm), ending with a WS row. Place sts on holder.

Upper Front

Return 96 (104, 114, 120, 132, 138) front sts to needle, if they are not already on the needle, and rejoin yarn with RS facing at left armhole edge.

Shape Armholes

DEC ROW: (RS) K1, ssk, work in patt to last 3 sts, k2tog, k1—2 sts dec'd.

[Work 1 WS row even, then rep the dec row] 4 (6, 8, 9, 13, 13) times—86 (90, 96, 100, 104, 110) sts rem. Work even until 49 (53, 59, 63, 67, 69) Center Panel rnds/rows have been completed from beg of chart (including set-up rnd), ending with WS Row 16 (4, 10, 14, 2, 4) of chart—center panel measures 5½ (6, 6½, 7, 7½, 7¾)" (14, [15, 16.5, 18, 19, 19.5] cm) from beg of chart; armholes measure 4 (4½, 5, 5½, 6, 6¼)" (10 [11.5, 12.5, 14, 15, 16] cm).

Shape Left Front Neck

NEXT ROW: (RS) Work 43 (45, 48, 50, 52, 55) left front sts in patt, M1, place rem 43 (45, 48, 50, 52, 55) right front neck sts on holder or allow them to rest on needle while working the left front neck—44 (46, 49, 51, 53, 56) left front sts.

Keeping new st at neck edge (end of RS rows; beg of WS rows) in St st, work even in patt until armhole measures 5¾ (6¼, 6¾, 7¼, 7¾, 8)" (14.5 [16, 17, 18.5, 19.5, 20.5] cm), ending with a RS row—front neck slit measures about 1¾" (4.5 cm) high.

BO 11 (11, 11, 11, 17, 17) sts at beg of next WS row, then BO 8 sts at beg of foll WS row, then BO 6 sts at beg of next WS row—19 (21, 24, 26, 22, 25) sts rem.

DEC ROW: (RS) Work to last 3 sts, k2tog, k1—1 st dec'd.

Work 1 WS row even, then rep the dec row—17 (19, 22, 24, 20, 23) sts rem. Work even until armhole measures 7¼ (7¾, 8¼, 8¾, 9¼, 9½)" (18.5 [19.5, 21, 22, 23.5, 24] cm), ending with a WS row. Place sts on holder.

Center Panel

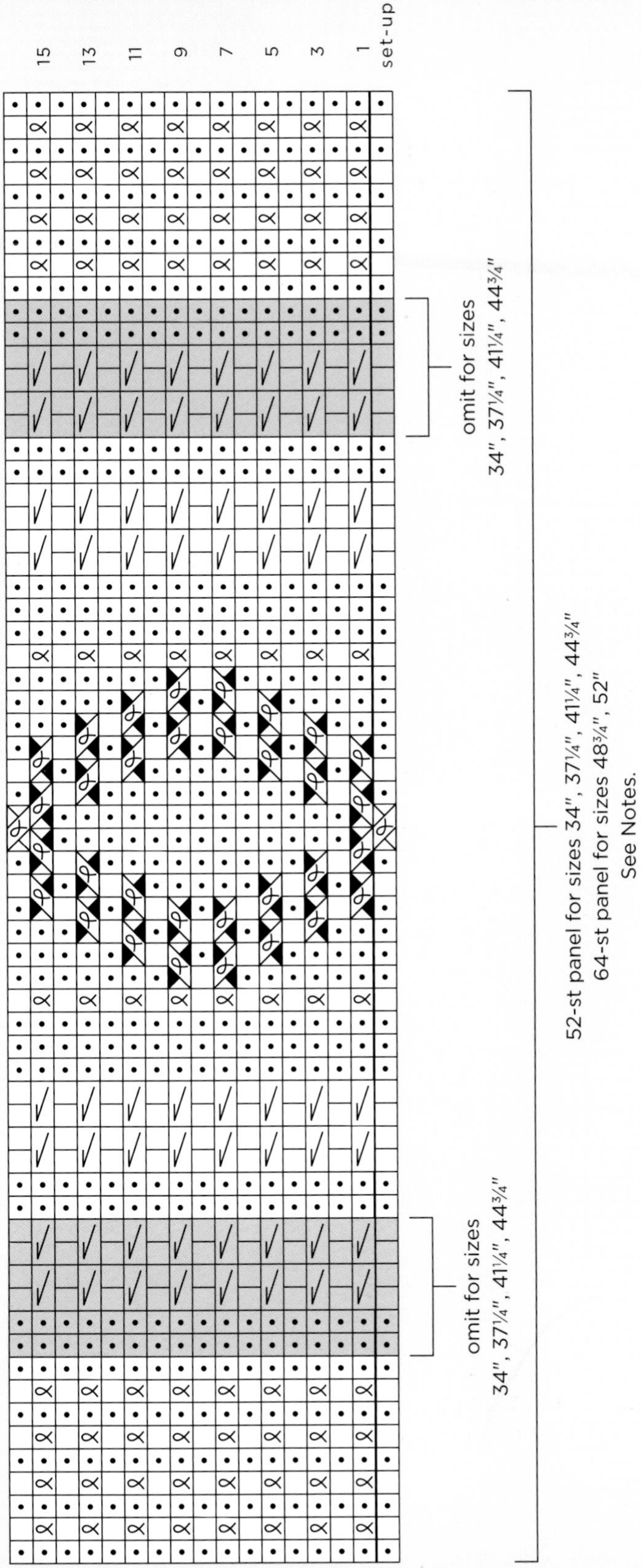

15
13
11
9
7
5
3
1
set-up
omit for sizes 34", 37¼", 41¼", 44¾"
52-st panel for sizes 34", 37¼", 41¼", 44¾"
64-st panel for sizes 48¾", 52"
See Notes.
omit for sizes 34", 37¼", 41¼", 44¾"

- knit on RS rows and all rnds; purl on WS rows
- k1tbl on RS rows and all rnds
- purl on RS rows and all rnds; knit on WS rows
- yo-k2-pass (see Stitch Guide)
- sl 1 st onto cn and hold in back, k1tbl, p1 from cn
- sl 1 st onto cn and hold in front, p1, k1tbl from cn
- on RS rows and all rnds, sl 1 st onto cn and hold in front, k1tbl, k1tbl from cn; on WS rows, sl 1 st onto cn and hold in front, p1tbl, p1tbl from cn

Shape Right Front Neck

Return 43 (45, 48, 50, 52, 55) held right front neck sts to needle, if they are not already on the needle, and rejoin yarn with RS facing at neck edge.

NEXT ROW: (RS) M1, work to end—44 (46, 49, 51, 53, 56) sts.

Keeping new st at neck edge (beg of RS rows, end of WS rows) in St st, work even in patt until armhole measures 5¾ (6¼, 6¾, 7¼, 7¾, 8)" (14.5 [16, 17, 18.5, 19.5, 20.5] cm), ending with a WS row—front neck slit measures about 1¾" (4.5 cm) high.

BO 11 (11, 11, 11, 17, 17) sts at beg of next RS row, then BO 8 sts at beg of foll RS row, then BO 6 sts at beg of next RS row—19 (21, 24, 26, 22, 25) sts rem.

DEC ROW: (RS) K1, ssk, work in patt to end—1 st dec'd.

Work 1 WS row even, then rep the dec row—17 (19, 22, 24, 20, 23) sts rem. Work even until armhole measures 7¼ (7¾, 8¼, 8¾, 9¼, 9½)" (18.5 [19.5, 21, 22, 23.5, 24] cm), ending with a WS row. Place sts on holder.

Join Shoulders

Block body to measurements. With RS touching and WS facing outward, use the three-needle method (see Glossary) to BO 17 (19, 22, 24, 20, 23) front and back sts tog at shoulders.

Sleeves

With RS facing, cir needle, and beg at shoulder join, pick up and knit 32 (34, 36, 38, 40, 41) sts evenly spaced along armhole edge to beg of underarm BO (about 1 st for every 2 rows), pm, pick up and knit 10 (12, 14, 18, 20, 24) sts across underarm BO, pm, then pick up and knit 32 (34, 36, 38, 40, 41) sts evenly spaced along rem armhole edge to end at shoulder join, pm—74 (80, 86, 94, 100, 106) sts total.

Sleeve Cap

Work short-rows (see Glossary) to shape cap as foll:

SHORT-ROW 1: (RS) K7, wrap next st, turn work.

SHORT-ROW 2: (WS) Purl to shoulder join m, sl m, p7, wrap next st, turn.

SHORT-ROW 3: K7, sl m, k11 working wrap tog with wrapped st, wrap next st, turn.

SHORT-ROW 4: P11, sl m, p11 working wrap tog with wrapped st, wrap next st, turn.

SHORT-ROW 5: K11, sl m, k15 working wrap tog with wrapped st, wrap next st, turn.

SHORT-ROW 6: P15, sl m, p15 working wrap tog with wrapped st, wrap next st, turn.

SHORT-ROW 7: K15, sl m, k16 working wrap tog with wrapped st, wrap next st, turn.

SHORT-ROW 8: P16, sl m, p16 working wrap tog with wrapped st, wrap next st, turn—last wrapped st at each side is the 17th st from shoulder join m.

SHORT-ROW 9: Sl m as you come to it, knit to previously wrapped st, work wrap tog with wrapped st, wrap next st, turn—wrapped st is 1 st farther from shoulder join m.

SHORT-ROW 10: Sl m as you come to it, purl to previously wrapped st, work wrap tog with wrapped st, wrap next st, turn—wrapped st is 1 st farther from shoulder join m.

Rep the last 2 rows 14 (16, 18, 20, 22, 23) more times—last wrapped st at each side is the st next to the m on each side of the underarm sts.

NEXT ROW: (RS) Knit to shoulder m, remove m, knit to wrapped st, work wrap tog with wrapped st, remove m, k5 (6, 7, 9, 10, 12) to center of underarm, pm for center of underarm.

NEXT RND: Change to dpn. With RS still facing, knit 1 rnd on all sts, working rem wrap tog with wrapped st and ending at underarm m—sleeve cap measures 4½ (5, 5¼, 5¾, 6¼, 6½)" (11.5 [12.5, 13.5, 14.5, 16, 16.5] cm) from pick-up row, measured straight up along a single column of sts in center of cap.

Lower Sleeve

Knit 4 rnds.

DEC RND: K1, ssk, knit to last 3 sts, k2tog, k1—2 sts dec'd.

Cont in St st, rep the dec rnd every 6th rnd 0 (0, 0, 9, 15, 15) times, then every 7th rnd 0 (0, 0, 4, 0, 0) times, then every 8th rnd 0 (4, 8, 0, 0, 0) times, then every 9th rnd 0 (5, 2, 0, 0, 0) times, then every 10th rnd 3 (0, 0, 0, 0, 0) times, then every 12th rnd 3 (0, 0, 0, 0, 0) times—60 (60, 64, 66, 68, 74) sts rem. Work even until sleeve measures 9½ (9½, 10, 10, 11, 11)" (24 [24, 25.5, 25.5, 28, 28] cm) from joining rnd.

INC RND: [K10 (10, 10, 11, 11, 12), M1] 6 times, k0 (0, 4, 0, 2, 2)—66 (66, 70, 72, 74, 80) sts.

NEXT RND: *K1, p2; rep from * to last 0 (0, 1, 0, 2, 2) st(s), k0 (0, 1, 0, 1, 1), p0 (0, 0, 0, 1, 1).

NEXT RND: *K1tbl, p2; rep from * to last 0 (0, 1, 0, 2, 2) st(s), k0 (0, 1, 0, 1, 1)tbl, p0 (0, 0, 0, 1, 1).

Rep the last 2 rnds until twisted rib measures 2" (5 cm) and sleeve measures 11½ (11½, 12, 12, 13, 13)" (29 [29, 30.5, 30.5, 33, 33] cm) from joining rnd. Loosely BO all sts.

Finishing
Collar

NOTE: The RS of the collar corresponds to the WS of the garment so that the RS of the collar will show on the outside when the collar is folded down.

With cir needle and WS of garment facing, pick up and knit 32 (32, 32, 32, 38, 38) sts evenly spaced along left front neck, 53 (53, 53, 53, 63, 63) sts across back neck, and 32 (32, 32, 32, 38, 38) sts evenly spaced along right front neck—117 (117, 117, 117, 139, 139) sts total. Work collar patt according to your size as foll.

Sizes 34 (37¼, 41¼, 44¾)"

ROW 1: (WS of collar; RS of garment) K1, [k1, p1] 2 times, k3, p1, k3, p4, k3, [p1, k1] 4 times, p63, [k1, p1] 4 times, k3, p4, k3, p1, k3, [p1, k1] 2 times, k1.

ROW 2: (RS of collar; WS of garment) K1, [p1, k1] 2 times, p3, k1, p3, [yo-k2-pass (see Stitch Guide)] 2 times, p3, [k1, p1] 4 times, k63, [p1, k1] 4 times, p3, [yo-k2-pass] 2 times, p3, k1, p3, [k1, p1] 2 times, k1.

Sizes (48¾, 52)"

ROW 1: (WS of collar; RS of garment) K1, [k1, p1] 2 times, k3, p1, k3, [p4, k2] 2 times, k1, [p1, k1] 4 times, p73, [k1, p1] 4 times, k1, [k2, p4] 2 times, k3, p1, k3, [p1, k1] 2 times, k1.

ROW 2: (RS of collar; WS of garment) K1, [p1, k1] 2 times, p3, k1, p3, [yo-k2-pass (see Stitch Guide), yo-k2-pass, p2] 2 times, p1, [k1, p1] 4 times, k73, [p1, k1] 4 times, p1, [p2, yo-k2-pass, yo-k2-pass] 2 times, p3, k1, p3, [k1, p1] 2 times, k1.

All sizes

Rep the last 2 rows until collar measures 2¾" (7 cm) from pick-up row, ending with a WS collar row. Knit 3 rows, beg and ending with a RS collar row. BO all sts kwise.

Weave in loose ends. Block again if desired.

Albero Cowl
JACKET

I love the versatility and easy wearability of cardigans. The substantial Aran-weight wool used in this design transitions the standard cardigan into a jacket. For a bit of interest, the edges are trimmed with reversible moss stitch, the button placket is offset to the side, and the generous collar fastens into a deep cowl. Waist shaping along princess lines adds a bit of subtle tailoring. To prevent possible stretching, the fronts, back, and sleeves are knitted separately and joined with stabilizing seams.

FINISHED SIZE

About 33 (36, 39½, 43½, 47, 52)" (84 [91.5, 100.5, 110.5, 119.5, 132] cm) bust circumference with fronts overlapped 2" (5 cm).

Jacket shown measures 36" (91.5 cm).

yarn

Worsted weight (#4 Medium).

SHOWN HERE: Malabrigo Twist (100% merino; 150 yd [137 m]/100 g): #56 olive, 7 (7, 8, 9, 9, 10) skeins.

needles

U.S. size 8 (5 mm): 24" (60 cm) circular (cir).

Adjust needle size if necessary to obtain the correct gauge.

notions

Markers (m); stitch holders; tapestry needle; nine ⅝" (1.5 cm) buttons.

gauge

17 sts and 23 rows = 4" (10 cm) in St st.

18 sts and 26 rows = 4" (10 cm) in moss st.

stitch guide

Moss Stitch (even number of sts)

SET-UP ROW: (WS; used for collar) *P1, k1; rep from *.

ROW 1 (RS) AND ROW 2 (WS): *K1, p1; rep from *.

ROWS 3 AND 4: *P1, k1; rep from *.

Rep Rows 1–4 for pattern; do not repeat the set-up row.

Moss Stitch (odd number of sts)

SET-UP ROW: (WS; used for collar) P1, *k1, p1; rep from *

ROWS 1 (RS) AND 2 (WS): K1, *p1, k1; rep from *

ROWS 3 AND 4: P1, *k1, p1; rep from *.

Rep Rows 1–4 for pattern; do not repeat the set-up row.

NOTES

» Because the larger sizes have deeper armholes, their lower bodies are worked shorter in order to keep the overall garment length (from lower edge to shoulder) from becoming too long.

» The fronts are asymmetrical. With the front edges overlapping by 2" (5 cm), the right front is about two-thirds the width of the back, and the left front is about one-third the width of the back.

Back

CO 72 (78, 86, 94, 102, 112) sts. Do not join. Work back and forth in rows as foll:

SET-UP ROW: (WS) P14 (15, 17, 18, 20, 22), place marker (pm) for dart, p44 (48, 52, 58, 62, 68), pm for dart, p14 (15, 17, 18, 20, 22).

Slipping dart m every row, work even in St st (knit RS rows; purl WS rows) until piece measures 4¾ (4¾, 4¾, 4½, 4, 4)" (12 [12, 12, 11.5, 10, 10] cm) from CO, ending with a WS row.

DEC ROW: (RS) Knit to first dart m, slip marker (sl m), ssk, knit to 2 sts before second dart m, k2tog, sl m, knit to end— 2 sts dec'd.

Work 7 rows even. Rep the last 8 rows 2 more times, then rep dec row once more—64 (70, 78, 86, 94, 104) sts rem; piece measures about 9 (9, 9, 8¾, 8¼, 8¼)" (23 [23, 23, 22, 21, 21] cm) from CO. Work even until piece measures 10½ (10½, 10½, 10¼, 9¾, 9¾)" (26.5 [26.5, 26.5, 26, 25, 25] cm) from CO, ending with a WS row.

INC ROW: (RS) Knit to first dart m, sl m, M1 (see Glossary), knit to second dart m, M1, sl m, knit to end—2 sts inc'd.

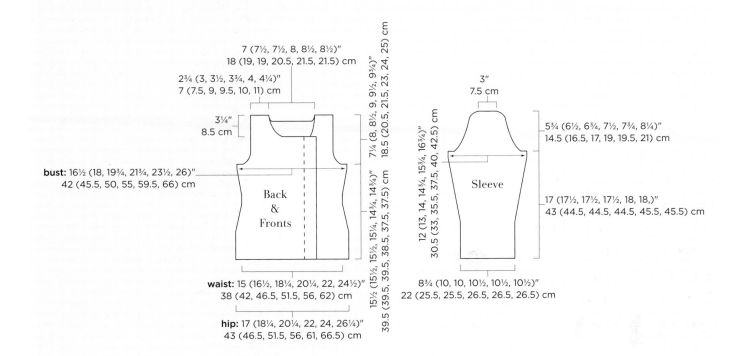

Work 11 rows even. Rep the last 12 rows 1 more time, then rep inc row once more—70 (76, 84, 92, 100, 110) sts; piece measures about 14¾ (14¾, 14¾, 14½, 14, 14)" (37.5 [37.5, 37.5, 37, 35.5, 35.5] cm) from CO. Work even until piece measures 15½ (15½, 15½, 15¼, 14¾, 14¾)" (39.5 [39.5, 39.5, 38.5, 37.5, 37.5] cm) from CO (see Notes), ending with a WS row.

Shape Armholes

BO 5 (4, 5, 6, 7, 8) sts at beg of next 2 rows—60 (68, 74, 80, 86, 94) sts rem.

DEC ROW: (RS) K1, ssk, knit to last 3 sts, k2tog, k1—2 sts dec'd.

Work 1 WS row even. Rep the last 2 rows 2 (4, 5, 6, 7, 10) more times—54 (58, 62, 66, 70, 72) sts rem. Work even until armholes measure 6¼ (7, 7½, 8, 8½, 8¾)" (16 [18, 19, 20.5, 21.5, 22] cm), ending with a WS row.

Shape Neck and Shoulders

NEXT ROW: (RS) K13 (14, 16, 17, 18, 19), BO center 28 (30, 30, 32, 34, 34) sts, knit to end—13 (14, 16, 17, 18, 19) sts at each side. Work each side separately as foll, allowing right neck and shoulder sts to rest on needle while working right neck and shoulder.

Left Neck and Shoulder

Work 1 WS row even.

DEC ROW: (RS) K1, ssk, knit to end—12 (13, 15, 16, 17, 18) sts rem.

Work even until armhole measures 7¼ (8, 8½, 9, 9½, 9¾)" (18.5 [20.5, 21.5, 23, 24, 25] cm), ending with a WS row. Place sts on holder.

Right Neck and Shoulder

With WS facing, join yarn to rem 13 (14, 16, 17, 18, 19) sts at neck edge. Work 1 WS row even.

DEC ROW: (RS) Knit to last 3 sts, k2tog, k1—12 (13, 15, 16, 17, 18) sts rem.

Work even until armhole measures 7¼ (8, 8½, 9, 9½, 9¾)" (18.5 [20.5, 21.5, 23, 24, 25] cm), ending with a WS row. Place sts on holder.

Right Front

CO 53 (57, 62, 68, 73, 80) sts. Do not join. Work back and forth in rows as foll:

SET-UP ROW: (RS) Work Row 1 of moss st (see Stitch Guide) over first 10 sts, k29 (32, 35, 40, 43, 48), pm for dart, k14 (15, 17, 18, 20, 22).

NEXT ROW: (WS) Purl to last 10 sts, work 10 moss sts.

Slipping dart m every row, cont in established patts until piece measures 4¾ (4¾, 4¾, 4½, 4, 4)" (12 [12, 12, 11.5, 10, 10] cm) from CO, ending with a WS row.

DEC ROW: (RS) Work 10 moss sts, knit to 2 sts before dart m, k2tog, sl m, knit to end—1 st dec'd.

Work 7 rows even. Rep the last 8 rows 2 more times, then rep dec row once more—49 (53, 58, 64, 69, 76) sts rem; piece measures about 9 (9, 9, 8¾, 8¼, 8¼)" (23 [23, 23, 22, 21, 21] cm) from CO. Work even until piece measures 10½ (10½, 10½, 10¼, 9¾, 9¾)" (26.5 [26.5, 26.5, 26, 25, 25] cm) from CO, ending with a WS row.

INC ROW: (RS) Work 10 moss sts, knit to dart m, M1, sl m, knit to end—1 st inc'd.

Work 9 rows even. Rep the last 10 rows 1 more time, then rep inc row once more—52 (56, 61, 67, 72, 79) sts; piece measures about 14¼ (14¼, 14¼, 14, 13½)" (36 [36, 36, 35.5, 34.5] cm) from CO. Work even until piece measures 15½ (15½, 15½, 15¼, 14¾, 14¾)" (39.5 [39.5, 39.5, 38.5, 37.5, 37.5] cm) from CO, ending with a RS row.

Shape Armhole

BO 5 (4, 5, 6, 7, 8) sts at beg of next WS row, work to end— 47 (52, 56, 61, 65, 71) sts rem.

DEC ROW: (RS) Work to last 3 sts, k2tog, k1—1 st dec'd.

Rep dec row every RS row 2 (4, 5, 6, 7, 10) more times—44 (47, 50, 54, 57, 60) sts rem. Work even until armhole measures 4 (4¾, 5¼, 5¾, 6¼, 6½)" (10 [12, 13.5, 14.5, 16, 16.5] cm), ending with a WS row.

Shape Neck

BO 24 (26, 27, 30, 32, 34) sts at beg of next RS row, then BO 2 sts at beg of foll 2 RS rows—16 (17, 19, 20, 21, 22) sts rem.

Work 1 WS row even.

DEC ROW: (RS) K1, ssk, knit to end—1 st dec'd.

Work 3 rows even. Rep the last 4 rows 2 more times, then work the dec row once more—12 (13, 15, 16, 17, 18) sts rem. If necessary, work even until armhole measures 7¼ (8, 8½, 9, 9½, 9¾)" (18.5 [20.5, 21.5, 23, 24, 25] cm) ending with a WS row. Place sts on holder.

Left Front

CO 30 (32, 35, 37, 40, 43) sts. Do not join. Work back and forth in rows as foll:

SET-UP ROW: (RS) K14 (15, 17, 18, 20, 22), pm for dart, k6 (7, 8, 9, 10, 11), work Row 1 of moss st over last 10 sts.

NEXT ROW: (WS) Work 10 moss sts, purl to end.

Slipping dart m every row, cont in established patts until piece measures 4¾ (4¾, 4¾, 4½, 4, 4)" (12 [12, 12, 11.5, 10, 10] cm) from CO, ending with a WS row.

DEC ROW: (RS) Knit to dart m, sl m, ssk, knit to last 10 sts, work 10 moss sts—1 st dec'd.

Work 7 rows even. Rep the last 8 rows 2 more times, then rep dec row once more—26 (28, 31, 33, 36, 39) sts rem; piece measures about 9 (9, 9, 8¾, 8¼, 8¼)" (23 [23, 23, 22, 21, 21] cm) from CO. Work even until piece measures 10½ (10½, 10½, 10¼, 9¾, 9¾)" (26.5 [26.5, 26.5, 26, 25, 25] cm) from CO, ending with a WS row.

INC ROW: (RS) Knit to dart m, sl m, M1, knit to last 10 sts, work 10 moss sts—1 st inc'd.

Work 9 rows even. Rep the last 10 rows 1 more time, then rep inc row once more—29 (31, 34, 36, 39, 42) sts; piece measures about 14¼ (14¼, 14¼, 14, 13½)" (36 [36, 36, 35.5, 34.5] cm) from CO. Work even until piece measures 15½ (15½, 15½, 15¼, 14¾, 14¾)" (39.5 [39.5, 39.5, 38.5, 37.5, 37.5] cm) from CO, ending with a WS row.

Shape Armhole

BO 5 (4, 5, 6, 7, 8) sts at beg of next RS row, work to end—24 (27, 29, 30, 32, 34) sts rem. Work 1 WS row even.

DEC ROW: (RS) K1, ssk, work in patt to end—1 st dec'd.

Rep dec row every RS row 2 (4, 5, 6, 7, 10) more times—21 (22, 23, 23, 24, 23) sts rem. Work even until armhole measures 4 (4¾, 5¼, 5¾, 6¼, 6½)" (10 [12, 13.5, 14.5, 16, 16.5] cm), ending with a RS row.

Shape Neck

BO 1 st at beg of next WS row, then BO 2 (2, 2, 1, 1, 1) st(s) at beg of foll 2 WS rows—16 (17, 18, 20, 21, 20) sts rem.

DEC ROW: (RS) Work in patt to last 3 sts, k2tog, k1—1 st dec'd.

Work 1 WS row even. Rep the last 2 rows 3 (3, 2, 3, 3, 1) more time(s)—12 (13, 15, 16, 17, 18) sts rem. Work even until armhole measures 7¼ (8, 8½, 9, 9½, 9¾)" (18.5 [20.5, 21.5, 23, 24, 25] cm) ending with a WS row. Place sts on holder.

Sleeves

CO 37 (43, 43, 45, 45, 45) sts. Do not join. Working back and forth in rows, work even in St st until piece measures 6 (6, 6½, 4, 3½, 3½)" (15 [15, 16.5, 10, 9, 9] cm) from CO, ending with a WS row.

INC ROW: (RS) K2, M1, knit to last 2 sts, M1, k2—2 sts inc'd.

Work 9 (11, 7, 7, 7, 5) rows even. Rep the last 10 (12, 8, 8, 8, 6) rows 5 (4, 6, 7, 9, 11) more times, then work the inc row once more—51 (55, 59, 63, 67, 71) sts. Work even until piece measures 17 (17½, 17½, 17½, 18, 18)" (43 [44.5, 44.5, 44.5, 45.5, 45.5] cm), ending with a WS row.

Shape Cap

BO 5 (4, 5, 6, 7, 8) sts at beg of next 2 rows—41 (47, 49, 51, 53, 55) sts rem.

DEC ROW: (RS) K1, ssk, knit to last 3 sts, k2tog, k1—2 sts dec'd.

Work 1 WS row even. Rep dec row on the next 2 (4, 4, 4, 5, 5) RS rows, then every other RS row (i.e., every 4th row) 4 (3, 3, 4, 4, 4) times, then every RS row 2 (4, 5, 5, 5, 6) more times—23 sts rem for all sizes. Work 1 WS row even. BO 2 sts at beg of next 2 rows, then BO 3 sts at beg of next 2 rows—13 sts rem. BO all sts.

Finishing

Using the three-needle method (see Glossary), BO shoulder sts tog at each side.

Collar

With RS facing and beg at right front edge, pick up and knit 38 (40, 41, 44, 46, 48) sts along right front neck to shoulder, pm, 36 (38, 38, 40, 42, 42) sts across back neck, pm, and 14 (15, 15, 13, 13, 13) sts along left front neck—88 (93, 94, 97, 101, 103) sts total. Work even in moss st for 1" (2.5 cm), ending with a WS row.

INC ROW: (RS) Work in patt to 1 st before m, M1, sl m, M1, work to 1 st before next m, M1, sl m, M1—4 sts inc'd; 1 st on each side of each m.

Work 9 rows even, working each pair of new sts into established moss st. Rep the last 10 rows once, then rep inc row once more—100 (105, 106, 109, 113, 115) sts. Work even until collar measures 7½" (19 cm) from pick-up row for all sizes. BO all sts in patt.

Block pieces to measurements. With yarn threaded on a tapestry needle, sew side seams. Sew sleeve seams, then sew sleeve caps into armholes.

Weave in loose ends.

Button Loops and Buttons

Mark placement of 9 button loops about ½" (1.3 cm) in from the right front edge, with the highest loop ¾" (2 cm) below the collar BO, and the rest spaced about 1½" (3.8 cm) apart. Using two strands of yarn, make 9 twisted cords (see Glossary) each about 4" (10 cm) long. Fold each cord in half, insert the ends through the right front from front to back at a marked position, and adjust the length so a 1" (2.5 cm) loop remains on the RS. With WS facing, tie ends in an overhand knot to secure the loop. Sew buttons to left front, opposite button loops.

Olivia
SHAWL

Spare and elegant, yet easy to wear, most of this shawl is worked in plain stockinette for a good mindless knit. The shallow triangular shape—achieved with increases that flank the center stitch every other row as well as increases at each edge every row—is perfect for draping over the shoulders or scrunching up around the neck like a scarf. Two deep tiers of a whimsical flower-and-leaf pattern end the shawl with a playful note, punctuated by a flirty ruffle that is added to the bind-off edge.

FINISHED SIZE
About 56" (142 cm) wide across top edge and 21" (53.5 cm) long from center of top edge to tip of lower point, after blocking.

yarn
Fingering weight (#1 Super Fine).

SHOWN HERE: Malabrigo Sock (100% superwash merino; 440 yd [402 m]/100 g): #803 ochre, 2 skeins.

needles
U.S. size 5 (3.75 mm): 32" (80 cm) circular (cir).

Adjust needle size if necessary to obtain the correct gauge.

notions
Markers (m; 4 in one color for patt rep, 2 in another color for center st); cable needle (cn); tapestry needle.

gauge
23 sts and 32 rows = 4" (10 cm) in St st, after blocking.

stitch guide

Make Bobble (MB)

Work ([k1, p1] 2 times, k1) all in next st—5 sts made from 1 st. Turn work so WS is facing, p3tog, p2tog, pass p3tog st over p2tog st as if to BO—5 sts dec'd to 1 st. Turn work so RS is facing, knit the bobble st, and cont in patt.

RC

On RS rows, sl 1 st onto cable needle (cn) and hold in back of work, k1, k1 from cn; on WS rows, sl 1 onto cn and hold in back of work, p1, p1 from cn.

LC

On RS rows, sl 1 st onto cn and hold in front of work, k1, k1 from cn; on WS rows, sl 1 onto cn and hold in front of work, p1, p1 from cn.

RPC

On RS rows, sl 1 st onto cn and hold in back of work, k1, p1 from cn; on WS rows, sl 1 onto cn and hold in back of work, k1, p1 from cn.

LPC

On RS rows, sl 1 st onto cn and hold in front of work, p1, k1 from cn; on WS rows, sl 1 onto cn and hold in front of work, p1, k1 from cn.

NOTE

» The shawl begins in the center of the top edge and is worked downward, with increases inside the garter-stitch borders and on each side of the center stitch to shape the triangle.

Shawl

CO 3 sts. Working back and forth in rows, knit 6 rows, ending with a WS row—garter rectangle 3 garter ridges high completed. With RS facing, pick up sts around 2 more sides of the rectangle as foll: Pick up and knit 3 sts along selvedge (1 st for each garter ridge), then pick up and knit 3 sts from base of CO sts—9 sts total.

ROW 1: (WS) K3, yo, p3, yo, k3—11 sts.

ROW 2: (RS) K3, yo, k2, M1 (see Glossary), place marker (pm) in center st color, k1, pm in center st color, M1, k2, yo, k3—15 sts; slip markers (sl m) every row as you come to them.

ROW 3: K3, yo, purl to last 3 sts, yo, k3—2 sts inc'd.

ROW 4: K3, yo, knit to m, M1, sl m, k1, sl m, M1, knit to last 3 sts, yo, k3—4 sts inc'd.

Rep the last 2 rows 37 more times, ending with a RS row—243 sts.

NEXT ROW: (WS) K3, yo, knit to m, sl m, p1, sl m, knit to last 3 sts, yo, k3—245 sts.

First Flower Tier

NOTE: The flower tiers are worked on a background of rev St st (purl RS rows; knit WS rows); keep the center st in St st and cont incs as established.

ROW 1: (RS) K3, yo, p2, pm in patt rep color, work Row 1 of Flower chart (page 131) over next 115 sts, pm in patt rep color, p2, M1, sl m, k1, sl m, M1, p2, pm in patt rep color, work Row 1 of Flower chart over next 115 sts, pm in patt rep color, p2, yo, k3—249 sts.

ROW 2: (WS) K3, yo, knit to patt m, sl m, work next chart row over 115 sts, sl m, knit to center m, sl m, p1, sl m, knit to patt m, sl m, work next chart row over 115 sts, sl m, knit to last 3 sts, yo, k3—2 sts inc'd.

ROW 3: K3, yo, purl to patt m, work next chart row over 115 sts, sl m, purl to center m, M1, sl m, k1, sl m, M1, purl to patt m, work next chart row over 115 sts, sl m, purl to last 3 sts, yo, k3—4 sts inc'd.

Rep the last 2 rows 10 more times, then rep the WS Row 2 once more, ending with Row 24 of chart, and removing patt m on last row—317 sts.

Second Flower Tier

ROW 1: (RS) K3, yo, p12, pm in patt color, work Row 1 of Flower chart over next 141 sts, pm in patt color, p2, M1, sl m, k1, sl m, M1, p2, pm in patt color, work Row 1 of Flower chart over next 141 sts, pm in patt color, p12, yo, k3—321 sts.

ROW 2: (WS) K3, yo, knit to patt m, sl m, work next chart row over 141 sts, sl m, knit to center m, sl m, p1, sl m, knit to patt m, sl m, work next chart row over 141 sts, sl m, knit to last 3 sts, yo, k3—2 sts inc'd.

ROW 3: K3, yo, purl to patt m, work next chart row over 141 sts, sl m, purl to center m, M1, sl m, k1, sl m, M1, purl to patt m, work next chart row over 141 sts, sl m, purl to last 3 sts, yo, k3—4 sts inc'd.

Rep the last 2 rows 10 more times, then rep WS Row 2 once more, ending with Row 24 of chart, and removing patt m on last row—389 sts.

NEXT ROW: (WS) K3, yo, knit to last 3 sts, yo, k3—391 sts.

NEXT ROW: (RS) K3, yo, purl to center m, M1, sl m, k1, sl m, M1, purl to last 3 sts, yo, k3—395 sts.

With WS facing, work p2tog BO as foll: *P2tog, slip st just worked back onto left-hand needle; rep from * until 1 st rem, cut yarn, and fasten off last st.

Edging

With RS facing, pick up and knit 399 sts evenly spaced along BO edge of shawl.

ROW 1: (WS) K3, *p1, k3; rep from *.

ROW 2: (RS) P3, *M1, k1, M1, p3; rep from *—597 sts.

ROW 3: K3, *p3, k3; rep from *.

ROW 4: P3, *M1, k3, M1, p3; rep from *—795 sts.

ROW 5: K3, *p5, k3; rep from *.

ROW 6: P3, *M1, k5, M1, p3; rep from *—993 sts.

ROW 7: K3, *p7, k3; rep from *.

ROW 8: P3, *M1, k7, M1, p3; rep from *—1,191 sts.

With WS facing, work p2tog BO as for main section of shawl.

Finishing

Block to measurements. Weave in loose ends.

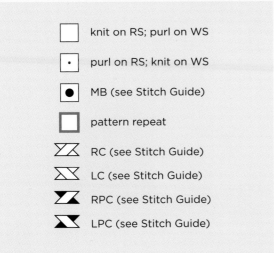

	knit on RS; purl on WS
·	purl on RS; knit on WS
●	MB (see Stitch Guide)
	pattern repeat
RC	RC (see Stitch Guide)
LC	LC (see Stitch Guide)
RPC	RPC (see Stitch Guide)
LPC	LPC (see Stitch Guide)

Flower

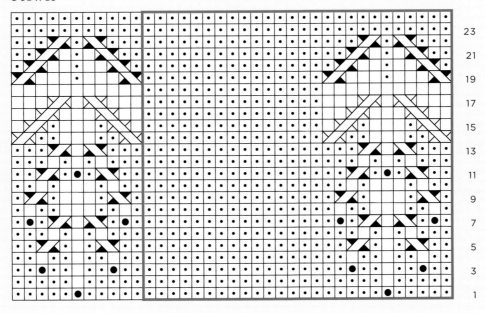

Gioielli
GLOVES

Inspired by a velvet bracelet cuff I saw at a local craft fair, these gloves are all about the deep ornate cuffs worked in smocking stitch. Because the smocking tends to draw in the fabric (it's sometimes used to cinch in waists), the cuffs are actually worked on more stitches than the hands. Given their simplicity, these gloves are great for showing off the beauty of hand–dyed, semisolid yarns. The yarn I chose from Schaefer Yarn Company is a practical blend of merino and nylon that will withstand the hard wear they're sure to get.

FINISHED SIZE

About 7 (7$^{1}/_{2}$, 8$^{1}/_{4}$)" (18 [19, 21] cm) hand circumference.

Gloves shown measure 7$^{1}/_{2}$" (19 cm).

yarn

Fingering weight (#1 Super Fine).

SHOWN HERE: Schaefer Yarn Company Nichole (80% extrafine merino, 20% nylon; 405 yd [370 m]/5 oz [140 g]): pomegranate, 1 skein for all sizes.

needles

U.S. size 3 (3.25 mm): set of 4 or 5 double-pointed (dpn), or 40" (100 cm) circular (cir) for working magic-loop method.

Adjust needle size if necessary to obtain the correct gauge.

notions

Markers (m); waste yarn for stitch holders; tapestry needle.

gauge

26 sts and 34 rows = 4" (10 cm) in St st worked in rnds.

Stitch guide

Smock (worked over 6 sts)

Insert right needle tip from front to back between 6th and 7th sts on left-hand needle, then draw a loop through to the front. Place the loop at the end of the left-hand needle, in front of the first st. Knit the loop tog with the first st, then work the next 5 sts as k1, p2, k2.

Smocking Pattern (multiple of 8 sts)

SET-UP RND: *P2, k2; rep from *.

RNDS 1 AND 2: *P2, k2; rep from *.

RND 3: *P2, work smock (see above) over next 6 sts; rep from *.

RNDS 4, 5, AND 6: *P2, k2; rep from *.

RND 7: (Note: The last smock of this rnd is worked differently in order to span the end of rnd.) P2, k2, *p2, work smock over next 6 sts; rep from * to last 4 sts, p2, skip the last 2 sts of rnd, insert right needle tip from front to back between 4th and 5th sts of next rnd and draw a loop through to the front, place loop in front of last 2 sts of rnd, knit the loop tog with the first st, work last st of rnd as k1, slip end-of-rnd m.

RND 8: Work last 4 sts of Rnd 7 final smock (first 4 sts of this rnd) as p2, k2, then *p2, k2; rep from * to end-of-rnd m.

Repeat Rnds 1–8 for pattern; do not rep the set-up rnd.

NOTE

» Both gloves are worked the same and can be worn on either hand.

Hand

Cuff

CO 56 (64, 72) sts. Place marker (pm) and join for working in rnds, being careful not to twist sts; rnd begins at little finger side of hand. Work set-up rnd of smocking patt (see Stitch Guide), then work Rnds 1–8 three times—piece measures about 3" (7.5 cm) from CO.

DEC RND: *K3 (2, 2), k2tog; rep from * to last 1 (4, 12) st(s), k1 (k4, k0), [k1, k2tog] 0 (0, 4) times—45 (49, 53) sts rem.

Thumb Gusset

SET-UP RND: K22 (24, 26), pm for gusset, k1, pm for gusset, k22 (24, 26) to end—1 gusset st between markers.

Knit 1 rnd even.

INC RND: Knit to m, slip marker (sl m), M1 (see Glossary), knit to next m, M1, sl m, knit to end—2 sts inc'd.

[Work 2 rnds even, then rep the inc rnd] 5 (6, 7) times—57 (63, 69) sts total; 13 (15, 17) gusset sts between markers. Work even in St st until gusset measures 2¼ (2½, 2¾)" (5.5 [6.5, 7] cm) from set-up rnd.

NEXT RND: Knit to first gusset m, remove m, place 13 (15, 17) gusset sts on waste yarn holder for thumb, remove m, use the backward-loop method (see Glossary) to CO 3 sts over gap, knit to end—47 (51, 55) sts.

DEC RND: Knit to 1 st before newly CO sts, k2tog, k1, k2tog, knit to end—45 (49, 53) sts rem.

Work even in St st until piece measures 3¼ (3½, 3¾)" (8.5 [9, 9.5] cm) from gusset set-up rnd.

Little Finger

SET-UP RND: K5 (6, 6), place next 36 (38, 42) sts on waste yarn holder, use the backward-loop method to CO 1 st over gap, k4 (5, 5)—10 (12, 12) sts total. Join for working in rnds. Work even until finger measures 2 (2¼, 2½)" (5 [5.5, 6.5] cm) from set-up rnd, or just below tip of wearer's little finger.

DEC RND: [K2tog] 5 (6, 6) times—5 (6, 6) sts rem.

Cut yarn, leaving a 10" (25.5 cm) tail. Thread tail on a tapestry needle, draw through rem sts, pull tight to close hole, and fasten off on WS.

Upper Hand

Return 36 (38, 42) held sts to needle(s). With RS facing, join yarn at gap next to little finger.

SET-UP RND: Pick up and knit 2 sts from CO st at base of little finger, knit to end—38 (40, 44) sts total.

Join for working in rnds. Work even for ¼" (6 mm)—hand measures 3½ (3¾, 4)" (9 [9.5, 10] cm) from gusset set-up rnd.

Ring Finger

SET-UP RND: K7 (7, 8), place next 24 (26, 28) sts on waste yarn holder, use the backward-loop method to CO 1 st over gap, k7 (7, 8)—15 (15, 17) sts total. Work even in rnds until finger measures 2¼ (2½, 2¾)" (5.5 [6.5, 7] cm) from set-up rnd or just below tip of wearer's ring finger.

DEC RND: [K2tog] 6 (6, 7) times, k3tog—7 (7, 8) sts rem.

Cut yarn, leaving a 10" (25.5 cm) tail. Thread tail on a tapestry needle, draw through rem sts, pull tight to close hole, and fasten off on WS.

Middle Finger

Return 24 (26, 28) held sts to needle(s) and join yarn with RS facing.

SET-UP RND: K6 (6, 7), place next 12 (14, 14) sts on waste yarn holder, use the backward-loop method to CO 1 (2, 1) st(s) over gap, k6 (6, 7), pick up and knit 2 sts from CO st at base of ring finger—15 (16, 17) sts total. Work even in rnds until finger measures 2½ (2¾, 3)" (6.5 [7, 7.5] cm) from set-up rnd or just below tip of wearer's middle finger.

DEC RND: [K2tog] 6 (8, 7) times, [k3tog] 1 (0, 1) time—7 (8, 8) sts rem.

Cut yarn, leaving a 10" (25.5 cm) tail. Thread tail on a tapestry needle, draw through rem sts, pull tight to close hole, and fasten off on WS.

Index Finger

Return 12 (14, 14) held sts to needle(s) and join yarn with RS facing.

SET-UP RND: K12 (14, 14), pick up and knit 1 (1, 2) st(s) from CO st(s) at base of of middle finger—13 (15, 16) sts total. Work even in rnds until finger measures 2¼ (2½, 2¾)" (5.5 [6.5, 7] cm) from set-up rnd or just below tip of wearer's index finger.

DEC RND: [K2tog] 6 (7, 8) times, k1 (1, 0)—7 (8, 8) sts rem.

Cut yarn, leaving a 10" (25.5 cm) tail. Thread tail on a tapestry needle, draw through rem sts, pull tight to close hole, and fasten off on WS.

Thumb

Return 13 (15, 17) held thumb sts to needle(s), join yarn to start of sts CO over thumb gap, pick up and knit 2 (2, 1) st(s) from base of sts CO over gap, knit to end—15 (17, 18) sts. Work even in rnds until thumb measures 1½ (1¾, 2)" (3.8 [4.5, 5] cm) or just below tip of wearer's thumb.

DEC RND: [K2tog] 6 (7, 9) times, [k3tog] 1 (1, 0) time—7 (8, 9) sts rem.

Cut yarn, leaving a 10" (25.5 cm) tail. Thread tail on a tapestry needle, draw through rem sts, pull tight to close hole, and fasten off on WS.

Finishing

Weave in loose ends. Block lightly.

Glossary

Abbreviations

beg(s)	begin(s); beginning	rev St st	reverse stockinette stitch
BO	bind off	rnd(s)	round(s)
cm	centimeter(s)	RS	right side
cn	cable needle	sl	slip
CO	cast on	sl st	slip st (slip 1 stitch purlwise unless otherwise indicated)
cont	continue(s); continuing		
dec(s)	decrease(s); decreasing	ssk	slip 2 stitches knitwise, one at a time, from the left needle to right needle, insert left needle tip through both front loops and knit together from this position (1 stitch decrease)
dpn	double-pointed needles		
foll	follow(s); following		
g	gram(s)		
inc(s)	increase(s); increasing		
k	knit	st(s)	stitch(es)
k1f&b	knit into the front and back of same stitch	St st	stockinette stitch
		tbl	through back loop
kwise	knitwise; as if to knit	tog	together
m	marker(s)	WS	wrong side
mm	millimeter(s)	wyb	with yarn in back
M1	make one (increase)	wyf	with yarn in front
p	purl	yd	yard(s)
p1f&b	purl into front and back of same stitch	yo	yarnover
		*	repeat starting point
patt(s)	pattern(s)	* *	repeat all instructions between asterisks
psso	pass slipped stitch over		
pwise	purlwise, as if to purl	( )	alternate measurements and/or instructions
rem	remain(s); remaining	[ ]	work instructions as a group a specified number of times
rep	repeat(s); repeating		

Bind-Offs

Standard Bind-Off

Knit the first stitch, *knit the next stitch (two stitches on right needle), insert left needle tip into first stitch on right needle (Figure 1) and lift this stitch up and over the second stitch (Figure 2) and off the needle (Figure 3). Repeat from * for the desired number of stitches.

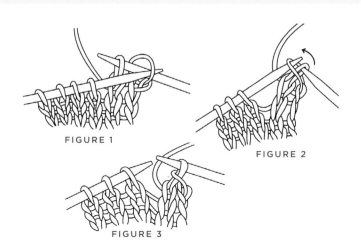

FIGURE 1

FIGURE 2

FIGURE 3

Sewn Bind-Off

Cut yarn three times the width of the knitting to be bound off and thread onto a tapestry needle. Working from right to left, *insert tapestry needle purlwise (from right to left) through the first two stitches (Figure 1) and pull the yarn through. Bring tapestry needle knitwise (from left to right) through first stitch (Figure 2), pull yarn through, and slip this stitch off the knitting needle. Repeat from * for desired number of stitches.

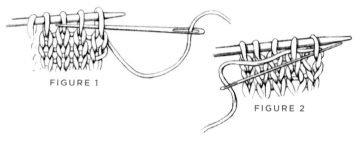

FIGURE 1

FIGURE 2

K2, P2 Sewn Bind-Off

See page 33.

Three-Needle Bind-Off

Place the stitches to be joined onto two separate needles and hold the needles parallel so that the right sides of knitting face together. Insert a third needle into the first stitch on each of two needles (Figure 1) and knit them together as one stitch (Figure 2), *knit the next stitch on each needle the same way, then use the left needle tip to lift the first stitch over the second and off the needle (Figure 3). Repeat from * until no stitches remain on first two needles. Cut yarn and pull tail through last stitch to secure.

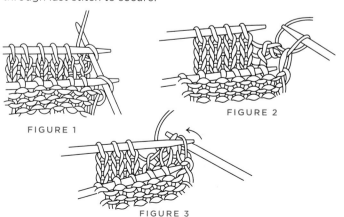

FIGURE 1

FIGURE 2

FIGURE 3

Buttonholes
Three-Stitch One-Row Buttonhole

Bring the yarn to the front of the work, slip the next stitch purlwise, then return the yarn to the back. *Slip the next stitch, pass the second stitch over the slipped stitch (Figure 1) and drop it off the needle. Repeat from * once more. Slip the last stitch on the right needle to the left needle and turn the work around. Bring the working yarn to the back, [insert the right needle between the first and second stitches on the left needle; Figure 2), draw up a loop and place it on the left needle] three times. Turn the work around. With the yarn in back, slip the first stitch and pass the extra cast-on stitch over it (Figure 3) and off the needle to complete the buttonhole.

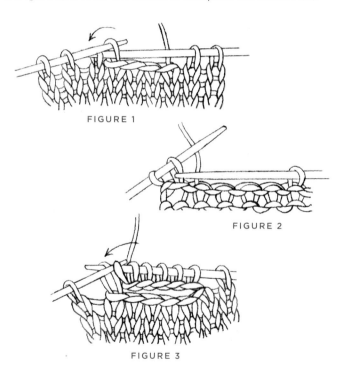

FIGURE 1

FIGURE 2

FIGURE 3

Cast-Ons

Backward-Loop Cast-On

*Loop working yarn and place it on needle backward so that it doesn't unwind. Repeat from *.

Knitted Cast-On

Make a slipknot of working yarn and place it on the left needle if there are no stitches already there. *Use the right needle to knit the first stitch (or slipknot) on left needle (Figure 1) and place new loop onto left needle to form a new stitch (Figure 2). Repeat from * for the desired number of stitches, always working into the last stitch made.

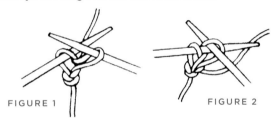

FIGURE 1   FIGURE 2

Long-Tail (Continental) Cast-On

Leaving a long tail (about ½" [1.3 cm] for each stitch to be cast on), make a slipknot and place on right needle. Place thumb and index finger of your left hand between the yarn ends so that working yarn is around your index finger and tail end is around your thumb and secure the yarn ends with your other fingers. Hold your palm upward, making a V of yarn (Figure 1). *Bring needle up through loop on thumb (Figure 2), catch first strand around index finger, and go back down

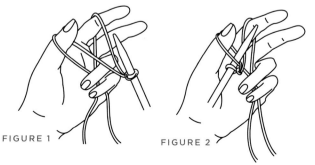

FIGURE 1   FIGURE 2

through loop on thumb (Figure 3). Drop loop off thumb and, placing thumb back in V configuration, tighten resulting stitch on needle (Figure 4). Repeat from * for the desired number of stitches.

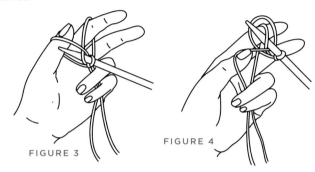

FIGURE 3   FIGURE 4

Provisional Cast-Ons

Crochet Chain Provisional Cast-On

With waste yarn and crochet hook, make a loose crochet chain (see right) about four stitches more than you need to cast on. With knitting needle, working yarn, and beginning two stitches from end of chain, pick up and knit one stitch through the back loop of each crochet chain (Figure 1) for desired number of stitches. When you're ready to work in the opposite direction, place the exposed loops on a knitting needle as you pull out the crochet chain (Figure 2).

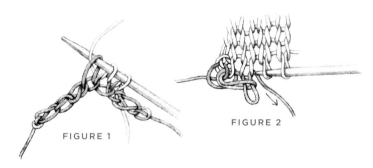

FIGURE 1   FIGURE 2

Invisible Provisional Cast-On

Make a loose slipknot of working yarn and place it on the right needle. Hold a length of contrasting waste yarn next to the slipknot and around your left thumb; hold working yarn over your left index finger. *Bring the right needle forward under waste yarn, over working yarn, grab a loop of working yarn (Figure 1), then bring the needle back behind the working yarn and grab a second loop (Figure 2). Repeat from * for the desired number of stitches. When you're ready to work in the opposite direction, place the exposed loops on a knitting needle as you pull out the waste yarn.

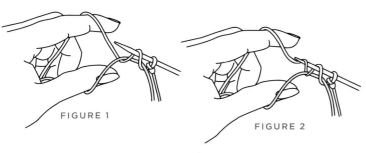

FIGURE 1   FIGURE 2

Tubular Cast-On

With contrasting waste yarn, use the backward-loop method (see page 138) to cast on half the desired number of stitches. Cut waste yarn. Continue with working yarn as follows:

ROW 1: K1, *bring yarn to front to form a yarnover, k1 (Figure 1); repeat from * to end of row.

ROWS 2 AND 4: K1, *bring yarn to front, slip 1 purlwise, bring yarn to back, k1 (Figure 2); repeat from * to end of row.

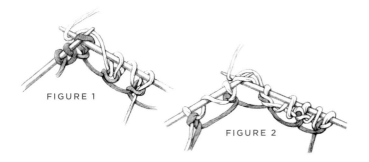

FIGURE 1

FIGURE 2

ROWS 3 AND 5: Bring yarn to front, *slip 1 purlwise, bring yarn to back, k1, bring yarn to front; repeat from * to last stitch, slip last stitch.

Continue working k1, p1 rib as desired, removing waste yarn after a few rows.

K2, P2 Tubular Cast-On

See page 33.

Crochet

Crochet Chain (ch)

Make a slipknot and place it on crochet hook. *Yarn over hook and draw through loop on hook. Repeat from * for the desired number of stitches. To fasten off, cut yarn and draw end through last loop formed.

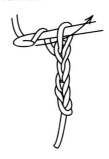

Single Crochet (sc)

*Insert hook into the second chain from the hook (or the next stitch), yarn over hook and draw through a loop, yarn over hook (Figure 1), and draw it through both loops on hook (Figure 2). Repeat from * for the desired number of stitches.

FIGURE 1

FIGURE 2

Decreases

Slip, Slip, Knit (ssk)

Slip two stitches individually knitwise (Figure 1), insert left needle tip into the front of these two slipped stitches, and use the right needle to knit them together through their back loops (Figure 2).

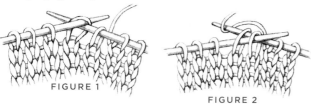

FIGURE 1   FIGURE 2

Slip, Slip, Purl (ssp)

Holding yarn in front, slip two stitches individually knitwise (Figure 1), then slip these two stitches back onto left needle (they will be twisted on the needle) and purl them together through their back loops (Figure 2).

FIGURE 1   FIGURE 2

Grafting

Kitchener Stitch

Arrange stitches on two needles so that there is the same number of stitches on each needle. Hold the needles parallel to each other with wrong sides of the knitting together. Allowing about ½" (1.3 cm) per stitch to be grafted, thread matching yarn on a tapestry needle. Work from right to left as follows:

STEP 1: Bring tapestry needle through the first stitch on the front needle as if to purl and leave the stitch on the needle (Figure 1).

STEP 2: Bring tapestry needle through the first stitch on the back needle as if to knit and leave that stitch on the needle (Figure 2).

STEP 3: Bring tapestry needle through the first front stitch as if to knit and slip this stitch off the needle, then bring tapestry needle through the next front stitch as if to purl and leave this stitch on the needle (Figure 3).

STEP 4: Bring tapestry needle through the first back stitch as if to purl and slip this stitch off the needle, then bring tapestry needle through the next back stitch as if to knit and leave this stitch on the needle (Figure 4).

Repeat Steps 3 and 4 until 1 stitch remains on each needle, adjusting the tension to match the rest of the knitting as you go. To finish, bring tapestry needle through the front stitch as if to knit and slip this stitch off the needle, then bring tapestry needle through the back stitch as if to purl and slip this stitch off the needle.

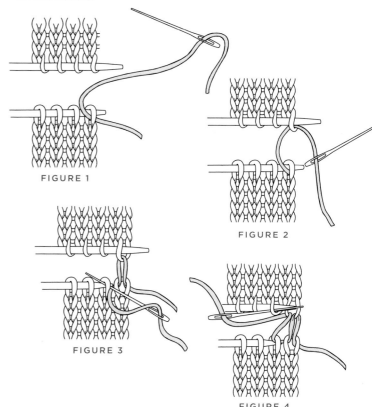

FIGURE 1

FIGURE 2

FIGURE 3

FIGURE 4

Increases

Raised Make-One

Note: Use the left slant if no direction of slant is specified.

Left Slant (M1L)

With left needle tip, lift the strand between the last knitted stitch and the first stitch on the left needle from front to back (Figure 1), then knit the lifted loop through the back (Figure 2).

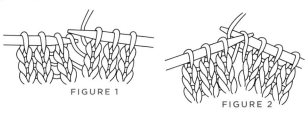

FIGURE 1

FIGURE 2

Right Slant (M1R)

With left needle tip, lift the strand between the needles from back to front (Figure 1). Knit the lifted loop through the front (Figure 2).

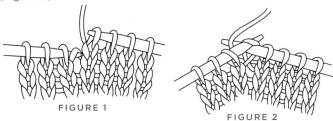

FIGURE 1

FIGURE 2

Purlwise (M1P)

With left needle tip, lift he strand between the needles from front to back (Figure 1), then purl the lifted loop through the back (Figure 2).

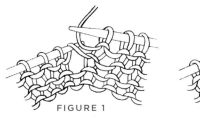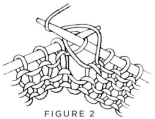

FIGURE 1

FIGURE 2

Pick Up and Knit

Pick Up and Knit Along CO or BO Edge

With right side facing and working from right to left, insert the tip of the needle into the center of the stitch below the bind-off or cast-on edge (Figure 1), wrap yarn around needle, and pull through a loop (Figure 2). Pick up one stitch for every existing stitch.

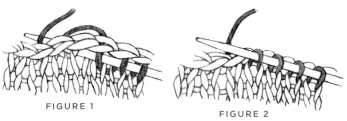

FIGURE 1

FIGURE 2

Pick Up and Knit Along Shaped Edge

With right side facing and working from right to left, insert tip of needle between last and second-to-last stitches, wrap yarn around needle, and pull through a loop. Pick up and knit about three stitches for every four rows, adjusting as necessary so that picked-up edge lies flat.

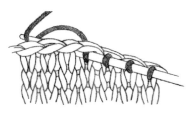

Pick Up and Purl

With wrong side of work facing and working from right to left, *insert needle tip under selvedge stitch from the far side to the near side (Figure 1), wrap yarn around needle, and pull a loop through (Figure 2). Repeat from * for desired number of stitches.

FIGURE 1

FIGURE 2

Short-Rows

Short-Rows Knit Side

Work to turning point, slip next stitch purlwise (Figure 1), bring the yarn to the front, then slip the same stitch back to the left needle (Figure 2), turn the work around and bring the yarn in position for the next stitch—one stitch has been wrapped and the yarn is correctly positioned to work the next stitch. When you come to a wrapped stitch on a subsequent row, hide the wrap by working it together with the wrapped stitch as follows: Insert right needle tip under the wrap (from the front if wrapped stitch is a knit stitch; from the back if wrapped stitch is a purl stitch; Figure 3), then into the stitch on the needle, and work the stitch and its wrap together as a single stitch.

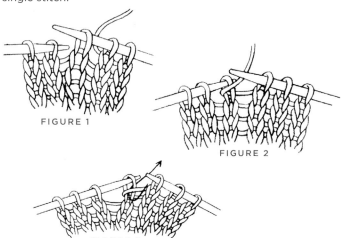

FIGURE 1

FIGURE 2

FIGURE 3

Short-Rows Purl Side

Work to the turning point, slip the next stitch purlwise to the right needle, bring the yarn to the back of the work (Figure 1), return the slipped stitch to the left needle, bring the yarn to the front between the needles (Figure 2), and turn the work so that the knit side is facing—one stitch has been wrapped and the yarn is correctly positioned to knit the next stitch. To hide the wrap on a subsequent purl row, work to the wrapped stitch, use the tip of the right needle to pick up the wrap from the back, place it on the left needle (Figure 3), then purl it together with the wrapped stitch.

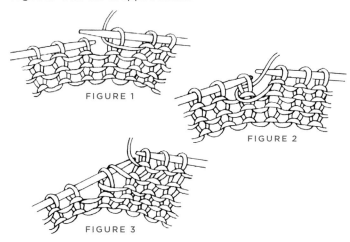

FIGURE 1

FIGURE 2

FIGURE 3

Twisted Cord

Cut several lengths of yarn about five times the desired finished cord length. Fold the strands in half to form two equal groups. Anchor the strands at the fold by looping them over a doorknob. Holding one group in each hand, twist each group tightly in a clockwise direction until they begin to kink. Put both groups in one hand, then release them, allowing them to twist around each other counterclockwise. Smooth out the twists so that they are uniform along the length of the cord. Knot the ends.

Sources for Yarn

Berroco Inc.
1 Tupperware Dr., Ste. 4
North Smithfield, RI 02896
berroco.com
in Canada: S. R. Kertzer Ltd.

Cascade Yarns
PO Box 58168
1224 Andover Park East
Tukwila, WA 98188
cascadeyarns.com

Classic Elite Yarns
122 Western Ave.
Lowell, MA 01851
classiceliteyarns.com

Diamond Yarn
9697 St. Laurent, Ste. 101
Montréal, QC
Canada H3L 2N1
and
155 Martin Ross, Unit 3
Toronto, ON
Canada M3J 2L9
diamondyarn.com

Fairmount Fibers/Manos del
Uruguay
PO Box 2082
Philadelphia, PA 19103
fairmountfibers.com

Karabella Yarns Inc.
1201 Broadway
New York, NY 10001
karabellayarns.com

Kelbourne Woolens/The
Fibre Company
915 N. 28th St., 2nd Fl.
Philadelphia, PA 19130
kelbournewoolens.com

Knitting Fever, Inc./Louisa
Harding/Sublime
PO Box 336
315 Bayview Ave.
Amityville, NY 11701
knittingfever.com
in Canada: Diamond Yarn

Lion Brand Yarns
135 Kero Rd.
Carlstadt, NJ 07072
lionbrand.com

Lorna's Laces
4229 N. Honore St.
Chicago, IL 60613
(773) 935-3803
lornaslaces.net

Louet North America/Gems
3425 Hands Rd.
Prescott, ON
Canada K0E 1T0
louet.com

Madelinetosh
7515 Benbrook Pkwy.
Benbrook, TX 76126
madelinetosh.com

Malabrigo Yarn
malabrigoyarn.com

Quince and Company
quinceandco.com

S. R. Kertzer Ltd.
10 Roybridge Gate, Unit 200
Vaughan, ON
Canada L4H 3M8
kertzer.com

The Schaefer Yarn Company
3514 Kelly's Corners Rd.
Interlaken, NY 14847
schaeferyarn.com

Index

Create smart knits

WITH THESE MUST-HAVE PATTERN RESOURCES FROM INTERWEAVE

THE BEST OF KNITSCENE
A Collection of Simple,
Stylish, and Spirited Knits
Lisa Shroyer

ISBN 978-1-59668-326-6
$24.95

KNITTING IN THE DETAILS
Charming Designs to Knit
and Embellish
Louisa Harding

ISBN 978-1-59668-256-6
$22.95

NEW ENGLAND KNITS
Timeless Knitwear with a
Modern Twist
*Cecily Glowik MacDonald
and Melissa LaBarre*

ISBN 978-1-59668-180-4
$24.95

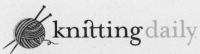